No Way!

Memoirs of J. Kenneth Lee, Esq.

Much Luck
J. Kenneth Lee

Winona Lee Fletcher

Editor And Ghostwriter

Outskirts Press, Inc.
Denver, Colorado

The opinions expressed in this manuscript are solely the opinions of the author and do not represent the opinions or thoughts of the publisher. The author has represented and warranted full ownership and/or legal right to publish all the materials in this book.

No Way!
Memoirs of J. Kenneth Lee, Esq.
All Rights Reserved.
Copyright © 2008 Winona Fletcher
V2.0

Cover Photo © 2008 Winona Fletcher. All rights reserved - used with permission.
Book cover credits: Cover design executed by Tim Revel of Revman Graphics, Nicholasville, KY 40356. It was inspired by a card sent to Lee at the height of his career as a Civil Rights lawyer in North Carolina.

This book may not be reproduced, transmitted, or stored in whole or in part by any means, including graphic, electronic, or mechanical without the express written consent of the publisher except in the case of brief quotations embodied in critical articles and reviews.

Outskirts Press, Inc.
http://www.outskirtspress.com

ISBN: 978-1-4327-2530-3

Library of Congress Control Number: 2008927568

Outskirts Press and the "OP" logo are trademarks belonging to Outskirts Press, Inc.

PRINTED IN THE UNITED STATES OF AMERICA

If I knew you and you knew me
If both of us could clearly see
And with an inner spirit divine
The meaning of your heart and mine,
I'm sure that we would differ less
And clasp our hands in friendliness.
Our thoughts would pleasantly agree
If I knew you and you knew me.

--J. Kenneth Lee,
A&T Register, January, 1942

Lee Entering A&T College as A Freshman

Table of Contents

Ken's Poem, 1942	iii
Table of Contents	v
Dedication	vii
Acknowledgements	ix
Foreword	xi
Preface	xiii
Confessions of The Editor-Ghostwriter	xv

PART I   1
LEE'S OWN VOICE: "Some Incredibly Important Trivia" with selected memorabilia from his personal, professional, philanthropic activities
    Ken's Tribute to Mama and Papa

PART II   59
LEE THROUGH THE VOICES OF OTHERS, Selected Memorabilia
    Introduction
    Family
    Old Friends' Letters and Sound of New Voices
    Cynthia (Bunny) McAdoo and the NCA&T Medal
    Tawanda Foster's (Miller) Poetic Tribute
    News and Record with Nancy McLaughlin
    Carolina Peacemaker with Kitty Pope

TIME AND PLACE FOR RELAXATION	99
FINAL CONFESSION	99

PART III   103
FOR VOICES OF THE FUTURE
    Lee's Letter to NC Central University
    Lee's Papers at UNC Law Library
    Lee's Collection in the International Civil Rights Center and Museum

Author's Bio   145

Dedication

TO NANCY, MIKE , MAMA AND PAPA, AND THE LEE SIBLINGS

Acknowledgements

To all those who contributed to the birth of this book--the family and friends of Ken, past and those of his present octogenarian days, WE GIVE THANKS.

The enthusiasm of those who agreed to add their "voices" to the volume sealed the decision to publish. Our gratitude overflows to:

Cynthia (Bunny) McAdoo, Atty. Tawanda Miller, Tanea Pettis at the UNC Alumni Association, Nancy McLaughlin and the *News and Record*, Kitty Pope and the *Carolina Peacemaker*, Amelia Parker and the International Civil Rights Center and Museum, The Staff at the UNC Law Library and all others who contributed to history by honoring Kenneth with awards and recognition.

To my daughter, Betty, in Maryland and my "other" daughter, Carol, in Michigan and to my special friend Betsy, the Archivist at CESKAA, whose expertise in the electronic world rescued me from the demons of digital ignorance more than once—Bless you all.

Then there was the professional help from Lynn Imaging and Tim Revel, Graphic Artist on the Kentucky end; the patient and willing Jennifer Rush at Outskirts and the accommodating staff at the Press--thanks for your expertise.

Love and gratitude to my friends and neighbors, Carrie and Gloria, and others who willingly "lent me their ears" when need arose to vent my frustrations and anxieties and to share my excitement as the pieces started falling in place.

Words of appreciation are difficult to find when friendships go back fifty-plus years, as in the case of Edith Griffin on the Greensboro end. She keeps the home fires burning when spirits [and bodies sometimes] falter. Without her as a conduit for electronic contacts with Ken, this process might never have come to an end. Thanks, with lots of love, Edith.

Winona--and Kenneth also.

Foreword

No Way! Memoirs of J. Kenneth Lee, Esq.

This is a book of how one man's efforts to break the chain of segregation changed the course of history in the United States. It is the story of how "some incredibly important trivia" experienced an "incredibly long gestation" before its birth in this volume.

The seed for this compilation was planted in an early 1974 letter written by an older sister (Lillian) to the nine surviving siblings of the fourteen children born in the H. F. Lee family from the union of Papa (Henry F., 1880-1947) and Mama (Sarah L., 1882-1942). The letter expressed Lil's desire to write a book that Papa always wanted on The Lee Family. As she was losing her sight to glaucoma, she wrote:

Not even the total loss of sight could blind me to the fact that I am the recipient of a special kind of love. I am persuaded to believe that this kind of love is not something of which we have laid hold, but rather something that has laid hold of us. Inspired by your love, and having so much time on my hands, I plan to gather material for a book on The H. F. Lee Family. . . In the near future, you will receive guidelines on your contribution, so start thinking.

Her letter stirred the writing fever in all of us. The youngest sibling (Winona) joined Lillian as writer and Editor. (Her task continues today alone as Editor and Ghostwriter.) Earlier, siblings were encouraged to be responsible for the form and substance of his or her chapter; to let the recounting of experiences be colored by the writer's own attitudes, circumstances, and development as a separate part of the whole family. The personality and individuality of the writer resulted. We had hoped the book would provide first-hand revelations of how one large, black southern family found life in America during the first 75 years of the 20th Century. We came to realize that some of our pens might well be capturing and preserving vital history even as we were living it.

The Chapter title of INCREDIBLY IMPORTANT TRIVIA was given in jest to the family humorist-- the youngest brother, J. Kenneth Lee. What the chapter revealed reached far beyond our expectations. It is time to let the man speak out.

Part One of this volume gives voice to an edited version of Kenneth's original chapter in The H. F. Lee Family Book. It also gives us glimpses of the man whose actions often spoke louder than his words as he set out to break down barriers and open doors.

Part Two provides a composite public picture of this surprisingly private octogenarian through those who knew (know) him and were (are) eager to preserve his legacy for posterity.

Part Three: Provides resources for future research and study.

Efforts by Lee himself to place his valuable materials in safe places.

Inventory of the J. Kenneth Lee Papers (1949-1994) in the Manuscript Department of the University of North Carolina Law School Library, Chapel Hill, NC.

Inventory of the J. Kenneth Lee Collections in the International Civil Rights Center and Museum (2004), Greensboro, NC.

Preface

J. Kenneth Lee has spent most of his 84 years saying 'NO WAY' to a world determined to set the course of his life:

When the one segregated school in his small hometown burned to the ground, thus, denying what was to be his graduation, he walked 5 miles to finish high school in a black church.

When his loving father, rebounding from The Great Depression and having to provide for a large family, handed him $34.00 (tuition) and suggested that maybe he should wait a while before starting college, Ken took the small gift, caught a ride to Greensboro and never asked for more.

> LITTLE DID HE KNOW THEN OF ALL THE WAYS
> HE WOULD BE FORCED TO SAY 'NO WAY'
> TO THE SEGREGATED SOUTH OF THE 1940's.

When Pearl Harbor changed his world and the Army threatened his carefree college existence, he joined the Navy and completed his under-graduate degree.

When the War ended, with both an engineering degree and a marriage certificate in hand he sought employment in all the local industries hiring engineers; he was told "TO GO NAWTH OR WEST." Replying "my roots are here," he created ways to support his young family by doing everything from selling wood to teaching at his alma mater. The pay was embarrassingly low.

When the black hospital where his beloved mother died in 1942 was about to be demolished in 1967 (in the name of integration), he knew he had to save it as a memorial to Mama. Successfully convincing the Presbyterian Economic Development Corporation (PEDCO) who provided the bulk of the money, he purchased the building, refurbished and converted it into a 100 bed skilled nursing home, primarily for indigent patients.

When he set his sights on a legal profession as a way out and found doors slamming one after another, he joined the NAACP suit to be admitted to the University of NC Law School, lived to win admittance, and passed the bar before his formal graduation in two and a half years. He was getting good at letting his actions say "NO."

He was flying high when he passed the examination to become a special agent of the FBI, but quickly plummeted when told he would be assigned to Detroit, New York or San Francisco. "Enough was enough," he said and with this response became a fearless Southern Civil Rights Lawyer. The world began to feel the force of his 'NO WAYS.'

Through threats and beatings to him and his family, bombings of his office and unvoiced sacrifices, he led the fight to tear down the walls that blocked freedom in education, business, housing, health care, entertainment and wherever he found unfair treatment. His 'NO WAY' was heard far beyond the South when he became Attorney pro bono for the four brave A&T students who refused to give up their seats at the Woolworth lunch counter in Greensboro.

    Much of Lee's fierce determination to open doors for himself and others has been concealed by his proclivity to work quietly undercover and to think ahead. He has, above all else, refused to leave the South.

Confessions of the Editor—
Ghostwriter, Confidant, Sister

As much as I hate to admit it, this is not my first attempt to publish a book on Ken's life. Earlier efforts were not successful, I must regrettably confess. Many events in both our lives prevented a publication from taking place. However, the discovery of a proposal written in 1989 encouraged me to move the desire beyond the proposal stage; thus, this book might be considered a "distilled" version of the original idea to write Ken's Biography. [Actually this effort has taken on a life of its own.] The reader is encouraged to envision the possibilities of a real biography enhanced by the opinions of others. Rereading the old proposal brought both tears and chuckles over some of the creative ideas flying out of my head at 4:30 a.m. [my best thinking time]. Pride, vanity and love for a brother that I've known for 81 years dictate that I must share parts of this early proposal with the readers. This might be a good place to prepare the reader for the many parenthetical and bracketed remarks [we call "asides" in the theatre] scattered throughout the text.

> Proposal for **LET THE MAN SPEAK: BIOGRAPHY OF J. KENNETH LEE** by Winona Lee Fletcher, 1989.
> Application for a grant from The National Humanities Center at the University of North Carolina, Chapel Hill.

"A common complaint of scholars studying the Afro-American experience is that Blacks have left too scant a historical record—written evidence such as diaries, memoirs, autobiographies. . . . This scarcity of personal records [is seen] as a particular handicap for Afro-American historians, and we have had to use ingenious and heroic devices to reconstruct the history of black people,"

These words of black historian Nathan Huggins have haunted me for some time, and since August my life has been overwhelmed by a sense of urgency to gather materials for a book on the life of J. Kenneth Lee. Lee's efforts to overcome the frustrations of being born Black in the segregated South has placed him on the "cutting edge" of history since he graduated, in 1952, as one of the first of two Blacks from a white school in North Carolina, UNC Law School. [In 2008, he is the only survivor.] While my interest dates back more than a dozen years, the urgency felt now can be attributed to several specific incidents of the past few months: 1) the summer publication of a book on the black man who integrated the schools of Kentucky and changed the course of history; 2) the discovery of a feature article on Lee (published in 1988 in the UNC Tar Heel) in which the now 93 year old former chancellor, Robert House, expresses candid attitudes reflecting those of a changing South; 3) Lee's decision to finally close his law office and to eagerly participate in my proposed project. The time has come when this story can and **must** be told. I propose, then, to research and write the J. Kenneth Lee story, or to assist as an amanuensis, if necessary, in the writing of a biography, or an autobiography of J. Kenneth Lee. The urgency to collect information from the many older participants is matched only by the necessity to be "on the site" where this history was being made—at The National Humanities Center at UNC, if possible.

J. Kenneth Lee was born on November 1, 1923, the 13th child of a minister father and a loving mother--very ordinary black southern parents. (I am the 14th and last of these children; 8 of the 14 survive.) As far back as the older siblings can remember, they observed signs that this child would develop into a most unusual man who would influence the course of history. In his 66 years of living in the South, Lee has, indeed, compiled an incredible record of involvements, achievements, and contributions.

Ten years ago, I researched and wrote Offshoots: The H. F. Lee Family Book (in collaboration with Lillian Lee Humphrey), a volume over 600 pages, self-published because of the prohibitive cost of such a profusely illustrated volume. Lee remarked in a chapter devoted to him: "My experiences at UNC would, undoubtedly, make stimulating subject matter that would benefit young Blacks today who take so many things for granted." There is much truth in this statement, although, the UNC story merely precipitated Lee's entrance into the annals of history.

[Then followed a recapping of Lee's achievements told elsewhere in this volume.] In addition to breaking down the barriers of segregation and providing legal representation for future leaders such as Jesse Jackson, Lee became an activator of and witness to numerous other societal changes [list follows in proposal]. Activities initiated by him have changed attitudes of both Blacks and Whites toward segregation, reform, and life in general in North Carolina and in the South; they continue to improve the quality of life for many, and to bring hope and faith when defeat and despair are much more likely options for many.

Scope: [A requirement of the application]

As envisioned, this book will track J. Kenneth Lee from his birth and early years in Charlotte and Hamlet, North Carolina through his introduction to Greensboro (by way of his entrance into college), the city "from which he refused to be driven"; the 40's and 50's when his years of service to his country were fraught with barriers and disappointments, the crucial decisions to fight the segregated South; his subsequent years of perseverance in the face of mental and physical abuse, discrimination, threats, bombings, shoot-outs, and close shaves with the Ku Klux Klan and the New Nazis; his failures and successes as a lawyer and self-made business man. The impact of his efforts will be explored in the continuum of the socio-political environment of the times, and an evaluative examination will be undertaken of the "monuments" to his commitment: The American Federal--first black-owned Federally Chartered, Federally Insured Savings and Loan in North Carolina which celebrated its 25th anniversary in 1984, Cumberland and Lincoln Grove Shopping Centers, products of urban development initiated by him; a 100-bed skilled nursing home care facility for indigent patients, a renovation project of the city's only black hospital in 1967—and the list goes on.

[Major changes have taken place in the conception and preparation of this book, as the reader will see. Other parts of this first proposal are no longer germane. The part that produced chuckles from both Ken and me as we exchanged ideas, reveals subtle traits of Ken and also of our relationship; some of these are shared here.

Ideas For Titles, Sub-Titles, Motivators For Thinking Aloud On Audio Tapes And For Writing In A Journal

From Wy, the Ghostwriter

Let the Man Speak
My roots are here to stay (inspired by the desire to stay in the South
Just like white students (from Daily Tar Heel, Jan 12, 1951) experiences at UNC.
Being Black and lucky, too (early childhood and praise for Mama and Papa)
Pulling the train without squeaking the wheels (from Mike's letter in the Peacemaker)
Flying above the crowd (on becoming a pilot; professional and personal use)
What does a black boy do with a degree in Engineering?
What if the Hen won't lay the egg? (subtopic for Delwatt experiences)
Paying the possum tax (inspired by your awful poem, your "colored sign from the Courthouse—never forgetting who you are.)
A dorm room? How 'bout a whole floor? (UNC experiences)
How many Baptist churches you know got "Bunsen Burners?" (early education, sacrifices, rewards etc.)
Were those my shoes that squeaked? (on dining room entrance/use at UNC)
Who asked to be first anyhow? (facts on the firsts in your life)
Go Nawth young man, go Nawth (using the cartoon sent to you as a springboard)
Mr. Lee, what's the Statute of Limitations on INJUSTICE?
'Nigra' loan – Maximum $13,500. Oh, yeah! (on negotiations with bank and getting your own started)
Becoming the fiddler and calling the tunes
Promises, Promises (on all the accomplishments not seen elsewhere)
Experiences I never dreamed of having—awards, recognitions, rewards, positions etc.
Far More with Much Less (family incidents with Mike etc.)

[Then followed a lot of questions for materials, interviews etc.]

Final Note: The proposal was rejected by the National Humanities Center at UNC and found a safe home in my files until now.

Part I
Lee's Own Voice

...He looked for and
found –SUCCESS."
J. Kenneth Lee
Poet Laureate
A & T, 1941

". . . I remember going to A & T with $34.00 that Papa had given me, along with the money I had saved from working with Henry and Alvis the two previous summers. I did not require any more money from home for my education after that day. . . .

I had encountered thousands of obstacles in life because of being Black, some I had been able to surmount, and some I had not. . . . I found it more difficult every day to completely divorce my thoughts from the possibility of Law School and getting involved in the civil rights struggle. . . .

I firmly believed that making money and doing good in the community were not necessarily inconsistent objectives."
J. Kenneth Lee

SOME INCREDIBLY IMPORTANT TRIVIA
John Kenneth Lee

I suppose one of the most insecure feelings I ever experienced in life came when it was my time to leave home to attend college. I had never been on my own before, and I wasn't sure that I could cope with the future alone. Sure there were a couple of summers away from home in Daytona Beach, but then I had Henry and Alvis to fall back on if any real problems developed. At any rate. I was determined to go because I wanted more than anything else to equip myself to be able to do something to make Mama more comfortable and happy. So many times, when things were a little tight, I had seen her insist that we go ahead and eat without her--that she would eat later. I would often go behind the stove when we had finished, look in the "warmer" which protruded above our wood cook stove, and it always made me sad when I would see what she had saved for herself, in comparison to what she had given to the rest of the family. My greatest ambition, therefore, was to be able one day to give her every material thing that she could possibly want. This ambition was never realized because Mama died while I was a freshman in college. Mama's death was the most traumatic incident to take place in my life from the date of my birth to this day, and has been responsible for most of the frustrations and personality changes that I have experienced. I was absolutely unprepared to deal with it at the time. That, however, is another story on which I could write an entire book, if it were not so personal.

At any rate, when time came to go to school, I was not sure of what I wanted to study. I had always been fascinated by the technical genius of Papa and his other sons, especially Alvis, whom I knew much better than the others because of the closeness of our ages. It seemed to me that Alvis could do anything with his hands and do it better than anyone else.

I was always proud of incidents like the miniature Marita Bread truck he had made from scraps and which the bread company had used for publicity for itself. I could never forget that when he was a very young teenager, he used to do odd jobs at the airport and some of the pilots would give him rides and lessons in exchange. When the local newspaper published his picture with the story that he was perhaps the first colored boy who had ever been awarded a pilot's license and certainly the first one in the area, I was the envy of all of my friends. This experience was responsible for my later becoming a pilot. I owned two Cessna 172's, the last of which I crashed in a South Carolina Senator's wheat field in Orangeburg. Miraculously, I escaped with only a few bruises, but that ended my flying career.

Anyhow, because of my fascination for the mechanical abilities of all the male members of my family, I decided to study Electrical Engineering at A&T College, Greensboro. There I came under the influence of A.C. Bowling, head of the Department of Electrical Engineering, and a man whose teaching and dedication were to have a tremendous influence on my life in years to come.

I remember going to A&T College with $34.00 that Papa had given me along with the money I

> ALL THE BOYS IN THE CLASS OF 1941
> L-R James Chunk Leak, J. Kenneth Lee, Rufus James, Elijah Griffin, Nathaniel Wallace, Thomas Jackson, David Douglas, Ceaser Smith

All the Boys in Lee's High School Graduation Class, Hamlet, NC

had saved from working with Henry and Alvis the two previous summers. I did not require any more money from home for my education after that day, but Mama and Papa were always sending me something; Papa would send a little printed religious tract two or three times a month, a practice which he continued, no matter where I was, until his death.

As soon as I got settled at A&T and moved into South Dorm, I went job hunting. My first job was as a pot washer at the old "Mecca Café," just across the street from the County Courthouse and the U.S. Post Office. I was hired by a headwaiter named "Otis" who had one of the most interesting senses of humor I have encountered. During a period of approximately one year that I worked there, I was never allowed in the dining room. I see Otis now fairly often and we always speak. I think he remembers me from somewhere, but I have never reminded him where. He has never lost his sense of humor.

School at A&T was pretty uneventful. Each issue of the school newspaper sponsored contests such as essay contests, naming a Poet Laureate for the campus etc. If you won, your picture, together with your submission, was published on the front page of the paper. I entered the first one with a poem about freshman initiation and won. Mama was so pleased when I sent her the paper that I entered and won each contest thereafter during my freshman year. After Mama died, I submitted no further entries; there was no more reason for winning.

No Way!

1959	Make & Model	Identification Mark	From	To	DUAL Received	Given
1-10-59	Cessna 172	4079F	Greensboro	Monroe	:	:
1-10-59	Cessna 172	4079E	Monroe	Charlotte	:	:
1-10-59	Cessna 172	4079E	Charlotte	Air Harbor	:	:
2-13-59	Cessna 172	4079E	Air Harbor	Local	:	:
3-7-59	Cessna 172	4079E	Air Harbor	Local	:	:
3-13-59	Cessna 172	4079E	Air Harbor	Albemarle	:	:
3-13-59	Cessna 172	4079E	Albemarle	Air Harbor (via Charlotte-Hickory)	:	:
5-2-59	Cessna 172	4079E	Air Harbor	High Point	:	:
5-2-59	Cessna 172	4079E	High Point	Air Harbor	:	:
5-10-59	Cessna 172	4079E	Air Harbor	Ral-Durham	:	:
5-26-59	Cessna 172	4079E	Air Harbor	Local	:	:

PILOT'S SIGNATURE

	TOTAL TIME ALL CLASSES	REMARKS:
	1:05	Solo X-C Tony Hammond RMT
	:25	Solo X-C
	1:35	Solo X-C
	:55	Solo X-C
	:55	Solo X-C
	:30	
	:35	Solo X-C
	:30	Solo X-C

Pages from Lee's First Pilot Log in Preparation for Learning to Fly a Cessna 172. Owned 2 Planes and Later Crashed Last One in SC Senator's Wheat Field, ending his "Flying Days." Lee Was Informed by a Servant that He Needed to Get Permission from the Senator to "Land" Here.

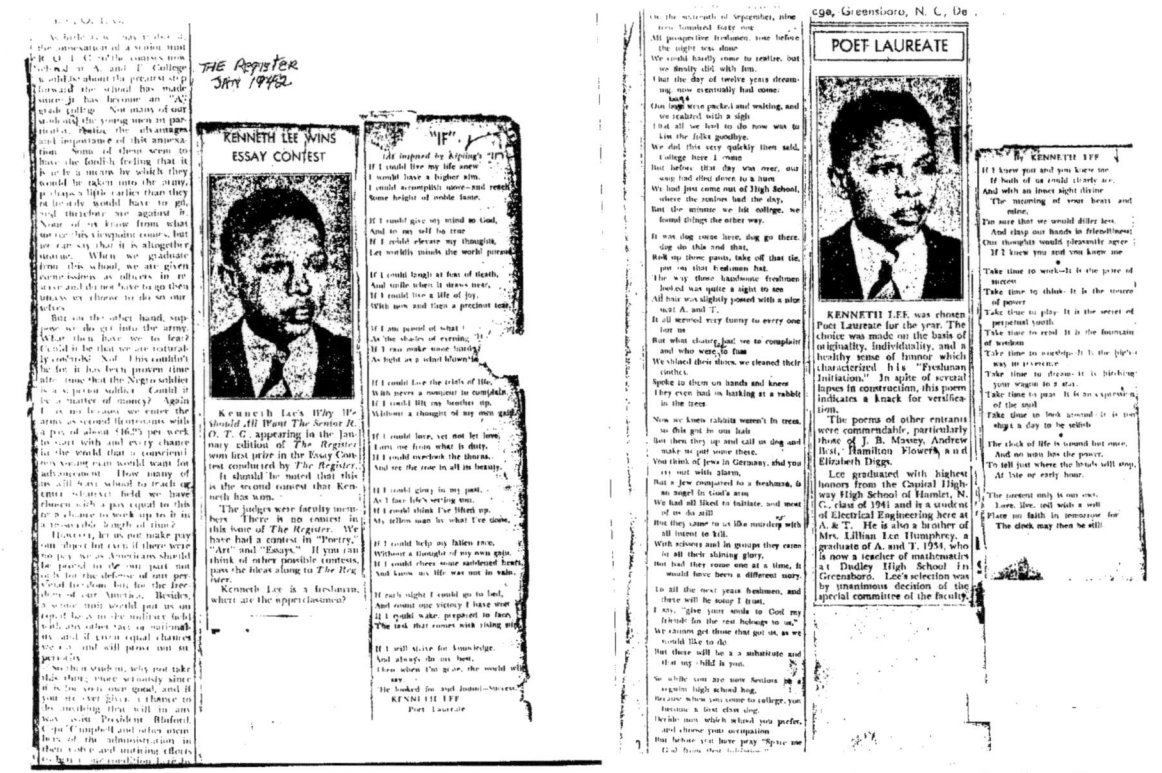

Fading Evidence of Ken's Writing as a Freshman at A&T

Nancy Young at Bennett College 1942. Lee's Wife in 1945

Aside from mostly routine work and study, I suppose the only real eventful things that happened to me at A&T was that I met Nancy Young, who was attending Bennett College and who subsequently " proposed to me" and became the mother of the world's finest son and the grandmother of three of the world's greatest grandchildren.

I completed the Electrical Engineering course at A&T in three years, although there is a five-year difference in the date of my entry and the date of my degree. About six weeks from graduation day, just as World War II was reaching its peak I was drafted into the Army, but to prevent going to the Army, I volunteered for the Navy for a two year stretch and served until the end of the war in the South Pacific. I was released exactly two years after I went in and, because of the influence of Mr. Bowling, was permitted to take up classes where I had left off, thereby graduating on schedule two years late.

After my degree, I tried to obtain employment in industry as an Electrical Engineer. Unfortunately, there was a problem that I had not heretofore considered. Despite the fact that Western Electric, Westinghouse, and all the other big companies in the area were running large daily newspaper advertisements for engineers, not a one of these potential employers would accept applications from anyone Black for employment in the area. I could easily have gotten work in the northern or western cities, but my roots now were in Greensboro and I didn't want to leave.

While in the Navy, I had taken advantage of the liberal continuing education program offered and had taken courses at the University of Hawaii, Pacific University, Hampton Institute and everywhere else that I had been stationed where there was a college that permitted Blacks to attend. I had also worked in the field for the entire two years in the Navy. I was, therefore, offered a teaching position at A&T immediately upon my graduation, and, after it became apparent that I wasn't going to be employed in industry, I decided to accept. I was offered a beginning salary greater than the salary that was being paid to Mr. Bowling, the Department head. Mr. Bowling had engineering degrees from Bucknell and Ohio State; had sat up and headed the department at A&T for 17 years, and had taught me everything I knew about electrical engineering. The ink was still drying on my degree, and yet, my starting salary was more than 10% greater than his. This is when I started my practical education on the inequities that life holds, but I did not have a solution to the problem. Shortly after this Mr. Bowling resigned.

I worked for A&T for three years, even though I was certain, after the first three months, that the classroom was not intended for me. This was just after the war and A&T had approximately three times as many applications as it had room for students. The classes were so large that it was almost impossible to be an effective teacher, especially since lab work was an essential part of all the courses that I taught.

After the first few months, the idea came to me that I should establish a school of my own and relieve some of the congestion. I talked with Curtiss Todd, the best lawyer I knew to handle the politics and paperwork involved, assembled the best engineers I knew, especially the one who had set up the veterans' curriculum at A&T, to handle the technical matters, and hired Wy who was just graduating from Johnson C. Smith University with a degree in English and who I believed was the best secretary to be found, even though she had had no formal training as a secretary. I found a large building in Winston-Salem and we "created" a college. We were trying to design an evening school to run from about 5 to 11 p.m. to accommodate working people—our potential students, and our teachers who were working at A&T. There were many problems involved in obtaining licenses and certifications from the State, the Veterans Administration etc., and we had no difficulty in surmounting all of them, except the problem of obtaining equipment.

We were to train radio, television and electronics technicians, and the cost of equipment to do this was tremendous. None of us had this kind of money and we found ourselves caught up in one of these "which came first, the hen or the egg" dilemmas The State wouldn't certify or license us unless we had the equipment, and the equipment manufacturers were happy to supply and finance the equipment for us—<u>after</u> we had the certification. But we didn't let this stop us for long.

Now that the Statute of Limitations has long since run out, the truth about our situation can now be revealed. We completed everything at the school, including the labs, except for the electronic equipment. We set the inspection date by state officials on a school break when no classes were being held at A&T. The night before the inspection, one of my partners, who also taught at A&T, and I rented a U-Haul truck, backed it up to the labs at A&T and transferred all the equipment from A&T to the school in Winston. When the state team made the inspection and started out the front door, we were already loading the equipment on the truck through the back door. Within about 18 hours after we started moving equipment out, it was all safely back in place and everybody breathed a sigh of relief.

The inspection team was so impressed with our elaborately equipped school that we had our certification back within a day or so. They said we looked just like a college. As soon as we got our certification, we put the exact same equipment back in the lab, only this time it was ours. Todd wasn't let in on the mechanics of how the certification was obtained since his "heart wasn't too good," but this is how Delwatt's Radio and Electronics Institute was born. A souvenir from our very first business venture, even before Delwatt's was recently found.

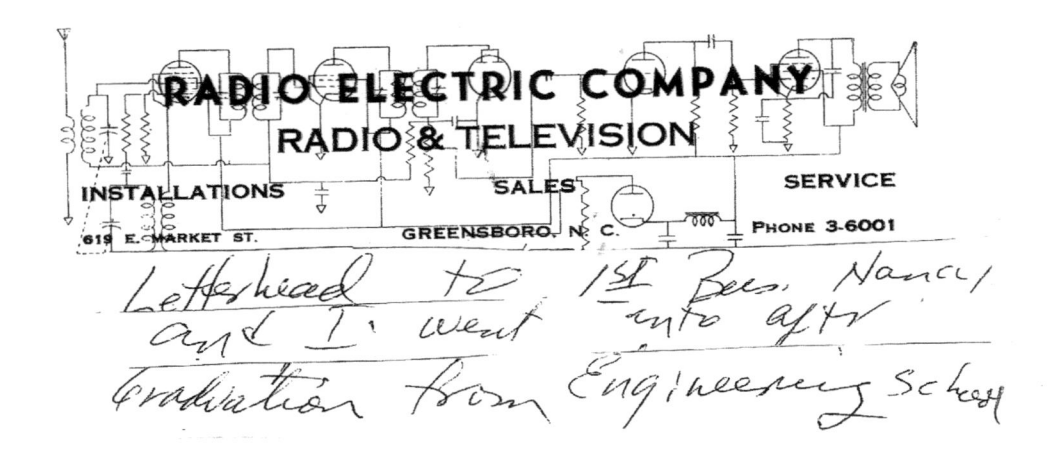

RADIO ELECTRIC COMPANY
RADIO & TELEVISION
INSTALLATIONS SALES SERVICE
619 E. MARKET ST. GREENSBORO, N. C. PHONE 3-6001

Letterhead to 1st Bees, Nancy and I went into after Graduation from Engineering School

At one time, we had approximately 300 students at Delwatt's and I made more money than I had ever made in my life. I had Delwatt's, the job at A&T and had opened the Ritz Theatre in Salisbury, NC, but I was still not satisfied with the kind of work I was doing and often found myself dreading the thought of going to work.

My daily association with Curtiss Todd had kindled some interest in the study of law, but there again, there was no adequate place to study law without going a long way from home; I never have wanted to do that. It was reflection time. I had been raised in a segregated society where discrimination and abuse were abundant, but where, for the most part, it had been accepted as inevitable. I had enlisted in a Navy and fought a war where there was not a single black officer in the entire Navy. When I went in the Navy, I was six weeks away from a B.S. Degree in Electrical Engineering with a good record. I applied for the Navy V-12 Program in Engineering at Ohio State University along with several white boys, none of whom had any college training. I saw them accepted, given a free college education and a commission while my application was rejected without an interview on the basis that the Navy did not permit the commission of Negroes into its officer corps. Some memories from the past kept flashing through my mind. One was especially vivid. It was how my first public recognition came when I was in the third grade and had recited my first poem in the school auditorium before the entire student body. It was entitled "Possum Tax" and I have never forgotten it in all the passing years. It went like this:

Lee in Boot Camp. He Enlisted in Navy to Avoid Being Drafted in Army WWII. Became a Non-Commission Officer, Electrician Second Mate

POSSUM TAX

Chile, dis nigger's seen some sights
   Scooting round on Saddy nights
Wunce I met de Ku Klux Klan
   Run plum in 'em, Lawdy man.
I was sho mer time had cum
   All dem ghosts struck me dum.
Couldn't er budge ter sabe me
      when
Wun ob de mos fo'mus men,
Ax me, stern like, "who yer am?"
   I des stood dar like a lam
But I answered might quick;
   "Ize Marse Johnson's nigger,
      Nick."
Den he grabbed mer arm an ax
   Has yer paid yer possum tax?"
Dat des skeered me plum ter deaft,
   But I sorter ketched mer breaf
And sed, "Yessir, cose I iz,"
   Den de wool des up and riz
Fur dat Ku Klux gunman sed;
   He am guilty - shoot him ded!"
When I heard dat wurd of doom
   Man! I didn't ax fur room
I des up and cut de dirt
   In de woods I shucked mer shirt.
I thanked Gawd mer nake back
   Wuzn't white, but good an black.
Then I heard a shot or two
   I des tried whut I could do;
An kep running lickty-split
   I ain't hardly stept it yit.
Nex day my young Marser, Ned
   Cum long by my house and sed
"Whur wuz yer, Nick, all las
      night?"
Den I rolled mer ayes up white
And sed: Marser, I wuz heer,
   Kibbered up Sur, hed and yeer."
You's a liah, Nick", he grinned
   But you ain't de fust dat's sin-
      ned.
Dat way - he laff an ax;
   "Has yer paid yer possum tax?"
Den I laff, too, long and loud
   I was so reliebed and proud.
Kaze I knowed he wuz de man,
   Grabbed me in dat Ku Klux Klan.
My Marse, Ned wouldn't hurt a flea
   Cose he warn't gwine ter shoot at me.
He des fired dat gun fer fun,
   Jes ter see dis nigger run!

No Way!

Not one person--teacher, student, or family had ever told me that I should not refer to myself as "Nigger" since this was what we were all commonly and publicly called by whites and what was generally accepted.

I had encountered thousands of other obstacles in my life because of being Black, some I had been able to surmount and some I had not. At any rate, I found it more difficult every day to completely divorce my thoughts from the possibility of law school and getting involved in the Civil Rights struggle.

At about this time, a group of students at North Carolina College Law School in Durham had filed a lawsuit to be admitted to the Law school at the University of North Carolina at Chapel Hill. At first no one took them seriously because the idea of black people going to school with white people in North Carolina was more than the average North Carolinian was able to imagine. However, those students were persistent, and as they began picketing the Governor's mansion etc. people started to take them seriously. Finally the lawsuit that was officially entitled, "Mckissick, *et al.* vs. Carmichael and that was being sponsored by the NAACP appeared to be becoming moot because the last of the original plaintiffs were now seniors at North Carolina College and apparently would be graduating before a decision would be forthcoming. The NAACP had spent almost a quarter of a million dollars on the lawsuit and was looking for someone to intervene as plaintiff to keep it from becoming moot. The plaintiffs were represented by Thurgood Marshall, now a Supreme Court Judge; Spottswood Robinson, now a Federal Appeals Court Judge in Washington; Constance Baker Motley, now an Appeals Court Judge in New York; Martin A. Martin, deceased of Virginia, and several others of the most prominent black lawyers in the United States. I talked with them and made the decision to intervene as a plaintiff in the case. What happened after that is a story in itself, but it resulted in my enrollment in the Law School of the University of North Carolina in the small group that marked the first time a black student had ever attended public-supported classes with a white student in the State of North Carolina. Harvey Beech and I were roommates at Carolina and even though there were five of us in the initial enrollment, two dropped out shortly and one finished later. Consequently, most of my experiences at Carolina were with Harvey Beech, whom I still hold as one of my closest and best friends.

L-R: Taylor, McKissick, Lee
(Taylor was Lee's first law partner. McKissick was in original
lawsuit for admission to UNC Law School and founded CORE.)

Lee and Beech with Chancellor Carmichael Prior to Registration at UNC

Lee, Beech and Lassiter Registering for the First Time at UNC

No Way!

University of North Carolina
Chapel Hill

STUDENT RECEIPT

No. B-1 6098   Date 8/31 19 51

Received from:

J. Kenneth Lee

For Account of:		
Student Fees & Charges		
Room Rent		
Room Deposit *Fall*	6	00
Application Fee		
Diploma Fee		
Board		
Swimming Privilege		
TOTAL	6	00

Cashier

DRIVERS PERMIT FOR PRIVATE VEHICLE
NAVBASE GTMO 5512/1 (REV. 3-63)

NAME: LEE John
STATUS: A/Civ
ADDRESS: DH-311
PERMIT NO.: LP-13-69
EXPIRES: 11-3-71
SIGNATURE: *J. Kenneth Lee*
SIGNATURE (BASE PROVOST MARSHAL): *C M Campbell*

ROOM ASSIGNMENT

Date June 12, 1951

(Name) J. Kenneth Lee has been assigned to Room No. 33 in Steele Dormitory.

Present this form to the Dormitory Supervisor for room key. Key will be issued in 02 South Bldg., from 2:00 to 5:00 P.M.

Approved

UNC Receipts for Room Assignment, 1951. Lee and Beech Were Assigned the Entire 4th Floor of Steele Hall

My experiences at UNC would, undoubtedly, make stimulating subject matter for a book that would benefit young Blacks today who take so much for granted. There is obviously not sufficient space here to tell that story. However, a few incidents had such an impact on my life and the subsequent lives of others, that they must be repeated here.

On our first day of enrollment, Harvey and I were stopped on the highway just outside Chapel Hill by a battery of highway patrolmen and news reporters. They escorted us on campus and were our constant companions for the next several weeks.

When we registered, we requested dormitory space. Despite the backlog of applications that Carolina had always had, we were assigned the entire third floor of one dormitory. I can recall the first time I went to the dining hall to eat, escorted by two big-armed highway patrolmen. There must have been five or six thousand students in there eating with the usual noise made by students in the dining hall at mealtime. When I came through the door, with the escort that had been assigned to me, a deathly silence fell over the entire room and this was the first time that I realized that my shoes squeaked. Before I graduated, I could have jumped up and down on the dining table and nobody would have missed a bite. This proves that people can accept change if they have to.

Lee, Lassiter, Beech, at Old Well on UNC Campus (Story goes that the Well later inspired the design for The Beech Park named in his honor in Kinston, his hometown.)

No Way!

Graduates of UNC Law Class on 1952 at 50th Class Reunion.
Lee and Beech (in wheel chair) in Front Row Center

We were admitted in 1950, and it was football season. Instead of being given tickets in the student section, we were given tickets in the section marked "colored" and located behind the goal post with adequate fencing and other devices to protect it from the other parts of the stadium. After protests to the Governor and Board of Trustees, the courts etc., we were finally issued tickets to the regular student section. In looking through old things recently, I was amused when I again read the cover letter that the Chancellor sent us with the tickets. He explained that football games were primarily for the alumni who would not take kindly to black folks mixing with white folks, especially while they were drinking, as they usually did at football games. This was followed by a kind of special appeal that while he was sending us the tickets, he certainly hoped we had sense enough not to use them.

I withstood the pressures there well, under the circumstances. I had trouble accepting without some bitterness the result the prejudices of others had on my family. My son, Mike, was about 5 or 6 years old then, and I still remember the time he became hysterical when he answered the phone and someone told him, using the vilest language possible, what they were going to do to his father.

The academic side of Law school at Carolina was something else again. I had, in my last years in high school in Hamlet, attended and graduated from school in a Baptist church with a class in each corner of the church. The high school for Blacks had burned to the ground and had not been rebuilt. We had no library, chemistry labs etc. and I could still remember the frustration I experienced when I first came to A&T and was enrolled in the chemistry class of Dr. H. Max Thaxton, the department Head who wrote the textbook. In one of his lectures, he had asked me to go to the lab and get a "Bunsen burner." I froze, since I had no idea what he was talking about. My first thought was to ask him: "How many Baptist churches you know got Bunsen burners?"

Well, this situation was magnified ten times at Carolina. I was thrown in with students whose prior training and opportunities were so superior to mine until there was absolutely no comparison. Most of them came from three or four generations of lawyers, while I had never been in the courthouse except for the time the UNC case was being tried. Students all around me were taking notes in shorthand, and a few in a specifically provided section, were taking their notes on a typewriter so they wouldn't have to transcribe them later.

I had had little need to study to get through school before, but this had suddenly come to a screeching halt. And, as if our academic deficiencies were not enough, seldom a day went by when we were not plagued with some racial incident that made it difficult to study. In spite of all of this, I finished law school in two years and one semester and passed the Bar before I graduated from school. I received a license before I received a degree, but I was not permitted to practice until after I completed the degree requirements. I was prepared for that; I was not prepared for what I discovered next.

After becoming a lawyer, I found that I was again saddled with some of the same problems I had had when I finished Engineering School.

I took the examination for a special agent with the FBI and passed. At the oral interview I was told I would be assigned to the, New York, Detroit, San Francisco or some other office since the FBI did not employ agents in the South except for special assignments where you had to be black to be effective. This was the last straw and since someone had at least implied that I was qualified to do so, I decided to join the civil rights struggle as a lawyer.

At this time, Conrad Pearson of Durham was representing the NAACP in all of its North Carolina cases, as Chief Counsel; I became assistant counsel. As such, I was local counsel in the first suit brought in NC to integrate the public schools; the first to integrate swimming pools, golf courses, and eating facilities in the South. Associated with me in these cases was always at least one

Lee in His First Office to Practice Law in Greensboro, NC, 1962

of the lawyers who had represented me in the UNC case. Consequently, I have had very close and intimate working relationships with the very best black legal talent this country has had to offer. Perhaps the greatest of these, in my opinion, was Charlotte Baker Motley. Not only was she an extremely competent lawyer, but also she was one of the finest persons I have ever known.

At one time during the sit-in demonstrations, I had more than 1700 active civil rights cases on the dockets of the North Carolina courts. I used to sit in the east side of the Greensboro jail with an A&T student named Jesse Jackson, now of Operation Push. I knew then that here was a young man who was destined to go far. Needless to say, no fees were paid for handling these cases in those days, only an occasional reimbursement of out-of-pocket expenses.

Representing criminal defendants in civil rights cases during those days was a hazardous occupation in every sense of the word, since these cases almost invariably involved alleged crimes by Blacks against whites. I can still recall the time I represented defendants in Carthage, NC, when seven black boys were charged with murder of a policeman by practically decapitating him with a shotgun. The first day in court, I noticed a farmer who appeared to have a stiff leg, and when he sat down, I saw the end of a double-barreled shotgun sticking out from under his trouser leg. These were uncertain times in North Carolina.

All in all, during my tenure as a civil rights lawyer, I represented 13 defendants who were tried for their lives. Fortunately, I have never had to answer the frustrating question "What else could I have done?" that many lawyers experience on a day of execution. Unless they have died of some other causes or been arrested for some other offense, all of the 13 defendants are free men today.

My career as a civil rights lawyer came to an abrupt end and my decision to terminate it was made in one day. It was near the end of the Woolworth sit-in demonstrations, when I was representing a group of A&T students whose goal was to integrate a local theatre in Greensboro. None of the theatres were integrated at that time. I had been involved with long and sometimes heated negotiations with the theatre owners, and the students had been involved in constant demonstrations. They were arresting the students by busloads, and since there was no place to put them, as soon as they were charged and released, they immediately returned to be arrested again. My son was among these students.

The owners finally decided that the problem would not go away by itself and they called me and advised that they had decided to give in and integrate the theatres. I was asked to meet with them to discuss the plan. The plan, as I recall it now, was that on that same day, they would give me 100 free tickets to the various theatres that I would give to the students less likely to start a riot so that they could attend that night. Thereafter, the number of tickets would be increased by 100 per day and the process repeated for 7 days to give the white public time to get used to seeing Blacks in the downstairs portion of the theatres. After 7 days, all restrictions of any nature would be lifted, and anyone who desired and could afford to pay could attend.

I was elated that after 175 years of segregation, I had finally been a part of bringing it to an end and that in just 7 more days it would forever be ended. I called a quick meeting of the committee of students working with me to give them the good news. We met and they sat silent while I outlined the plan. When I had finished, one of them dryly asked: "Mr. Lee, what's the Statute of Limitations on injustice?" I had no idea what he meant and asked him to explain. He did. He said: "We have waited almost 175 years and we're tired of waiting. We want integration TODAY, not 7 days from today."

I was shocked because in my mind, I had thought that I had accomplished a victory. It was a victory by the standards to which I had been accustomed, but changes in the 60's moved so rapidly that these young people were not at all enthused by promises.

I left the meeting without an agreement that the demonstrations would stop and met again with the theatre owners to advise them of what had happened. With little or no discussion, they agreed to instantly and unconditionally integrate the theatres and the controversy ended. Had I been as adamant in my prior negotiations as the students, I could have achieved the same results.

That same day I took a complete inventory of myself and decided that the Civil Rights Movement had outgrown me and since, as a result of our earlier efforts, there were now several young lawyers entering the field, it was time for me to step down. I did, and when I completed my pending cases, I did not accept any more civil rights cases. I had always felt that there were many other areas that needed attention now that segregation, at least by law, was no longer a way of life in the South.

After leaving the active area of civil rights, I started looking for areas in the law that would permit me to make money while still improving the economic plight of the people I represented. I was becoming more and more convinced that "black power" needed "green power" to back it up. Furthermore, I firmly believed that making money and doing good in the community were not necessarily inconsistent objectives.

Toward the end of 1957, the only piece of property I had ever owned was my home on Lindsay Street for which I had paid $4,800 when it was brand new. I had, however, been thrifty and had saved most of the money I had made, always with the idea of some day building a beautiful home for my family. I had known for years exactly where I wanted to locate the house and had reserved four corner lots at the location from the owner who was a client and friend of mine and for whom I had developed the entire subdivision. She sold me the lots for $2500 each or a total of $10,000 for the four. This was practically a gift as adjacent property was selling for many times this amount.

Finally the day came. I had paid for my lots, had completed the plans and working drawings for my house and had more than $35,000 in cash in my building fund. New houses were being sold for between $7 and $8 per sq. ft. The house, even in those days, was to cost more than $65,000, but with my equity in the land and the money I saved, I never dreamed I would encounter any problems in borrowing $25,000, especially since I had guarded my credit reputation to keep it perfect. After all, I was only seeking to borrow about 35% of the value of the property.

Since each major move in my life had been met with major barriers, I should have known that this decision would be no different. Yet, I was actually surprised when I went to a local lending institution and its officer refused to look at the plan or even discuss the loan. I was advised, in 1957, mind you, that it was the policy of all the lending institutions in Guilford County to limit home loans on "colored people" to $13,500, regardless of the value of the property or the borrower's ability to pay. One officer explained that the company thought I was all right personally, but he added: "Suppose something happened to you? How many "Nigras" could afford house payments such as these and certainly no whites would locate in the area." This information startled me since I had never had any reason to give it a thought before. However, to verify it, Attorney Major High, who was working with me then, agreed to help me check it out. We checked every single loan at the courthouse that had been made to Blacks for the past two years in Guilford County, one of North Carolina's most populous counties. Much to our surprise, there was not a single loan above this $13,500. It was suddenly reflection time again!

Fact: There were no black owned savings and loan associations in the entire state that were chartered by the federal government and only one, Mutual Savings in Durham, that was chartered by the State. Result: Whites could get together and set any limits they desired on Blacks who had no choice but to accept those decisions. The guy that paid the fiddler was again calling the tunes.

Ken Standing in Front of Federal Savings and Loan Building (Founded by Lee and others to serve the black community when other banks refused to grant loans over $13,500 to Blacks.)

It was then I started out to obtain a federal savings and loan charter. We were successful in organizing "American Federal Savings and Loan Association" in Greensboro, still the only federally chartered savings and loan in North Carolina and one of only two of any kind in the State. We opened in March 1959, with capital of $350,000. Seventeen years later, AFS&L lists assets of more than $10,000,000 and is still growing.

Immediately after the granting of the charter was announced, the other institutions lifted the restrictions and began making loans to all people on the same basis. Today, Greensboro has some of the most beautiful black owned homes of any city of its size in the South. I like to think that I made some contribution to this. New challenges remained, however.

During the late 1950's and early 1960's, Greensboro became involved in a new federal program that had been labeled "Urban Renewal." It was the first city in North Carolina to become involved and its first two projects were known as the "Cumberland" project and the "Washington I" project. These two projects resulted in displacement of 104 black businesses on both sides of Market Street and practically all of the land occupied by Blacks from A&T College on the north side of East Market Street to downtown and from Bennett College on the south side of East Market to downtown. While, admittedly, this property could be classified as slums, it still contained about 80% of all black businesses in the City of Greensboro.

The theory of Urban Renewal was that the slums were to be condemned by the City, torn down and new streets and facilities put in the area with other improvements that would forever eliminate slums. The land would then again be offered for sale to the displaced persons who could build new businesses and the lot of the poor Black would be enhanced. It didn't quite work this way in Greensboro. Instead of the displaced businesses being able to repurchase the land, almost all of the land in the Washington I project was obtained for the purpose of building a new main post office and one of the largest regional mail terminals that had ever been constructed. Of the 104 black businesses displaced, only two had been able to relocate in the Cumberland project, and these were two funeral homes that had been displaced. To me they were symbols of the demise of the 104 black businesses in the city. By this time, there were only two tracts of land left in the Cumberland project and none in the Washington I project. One of the tracts was a large one zoned for a shopping center and the other zoned for an office-building complex.

Because of the vast areas and the even vaster prices of these two pieces of land, it seemed that there were no Blacks even interested in seeking acquisition of them. One ugly fact remained; 80% of the black businesses that Greensboro had formerly had were gone for good.

Somehow I knew that this was not the kind of thing for which Papa and Mama and all Blacks like them had made all those sacrifices. Despite the fact that they were not here to receive their rewards, I felt compelled to do something. I made an agreement with two outside investors that if they would purchase the land, I would obtain leases, finance and completely develop the property without further expenses to them. We would then be partners in the completed project. This agreement resulted in the development of the "Cumberland Shopping Center" and the "Cumberland Office Building." The shopping center had key or major tenants consisting of Gulf Oil Corporation, A&P, Banner Machinery Corporation, American Federal Savings and Loan, plus as many small black businesses as size would permit us to relocate. The office building opened with tenants that included five physicians, a drug store, six lawyers, an architect, two insurance companies, two real estate agencies and a trading stamp company.

Directly across the street from these properties is located "Cumberland Courts," the very first housing project built in the United States under Section 221(D)(3) of the Federal Housing Act. It contains approximately 280 units of subsidized housing and it was my responsibility to acquire it for

President of UNC with Lee and Son, Michael, in Recognition of Michaels' Completion of Law School at NC Central, the Black School His Father Left to Integrate UNC Law School

St. James Baptist Church which now operates it.

Recently, I sold most of my interests in these properties and, at this writing, am in the process of moving into a new building with my son, who I am proud to say, is now, himself practicing law.

By the mid 1960's, I had begun to earn a very respectable income and had made several investments that had proven to be quite successful. It was about this time that Greensboro decided to build a new modern hospital and abandon the old L. Richardson Memorial Hospital that had been built and occupied in the 1930's.

Mama had spent her last days in the L. Richardson Hospital and I had always had a sad feeling when passing or visiting it. When the hospital moved out, I began to wonder what would happen to the building. I discussed the possibility of its purchase and rehabilitation with two of my investor friends, one who is President and General Manager of an NBA basketball team. The thought of it being demolished haunted me. Maybe it could become a kind of memorial to Mama.

As a result of this kind of thinking, we purchased the hospital, borrowed $300,000 from SBA and $300,000 from the National Presbyterian Church (PEDCO) and completely refurbished the hospital and converted it into a 100 bed skilled nursing home. In 1968 or 69, I bought out the interest of my partners and started operating the home 100% for indigent or welfare patients who could not pay for care in private nursing homes. I operated the facility until 1970 when it was leased to an operating company while I retained ownership of the property. The provision of the lease, however, provides that it is to be operated for the benefit of indigent patients and at no time has the occupancy ration contained less than 98% indigent patients. The home keeps a waiting list and I am advised that it is the third largest supplier of services to indigent patients in the entire state of North Carolina.

The operation of the home has not been at a loss to me, although it would be substantially more profitable if it were filled with private paying patients. I know, however, to make it available to people who cannot pay their own way is somehow more a tribute to Mama who made her last worldly sacrifices there.

L. Richardson Memorial Hospital After Restoration Initiated by Lee and Others. The Black Hospital, Slated to Be Razed in the Name of Integration, Was the Hospital Where Mama Lee Died. It was Converted into A 100 Bed Nursing Home for Indigent Patients

During my career, I have had many and varied experiences that I never dreamed, as a boy growing up in Hamlet, that I would ever have. I have met and shaken hands with every United States President since Harry Truman; have been appointed by the Attorney General of the United States and served as Special Hearing Officer for the United States Department of Justice; have served on the Board of Directors or Trustees of banks, two colleges, a church, and numerous corporations; I have served, and am now serving, by appointment of the Governor, as the only black State Banking Commissioner the State of North Carolina has ever had in its history. My life has been, and is now, a rich and rewarding one.

(Three sample certificates follow.)

Kenneth Lee, Local black attorney, has been appointed to the six-member Office of Minority Business Enterprise Advisory Board selected this week by Gov. James Holshouser. Lee has degrees from A&T State University and UNC-CH. He is president of American Federal Savings and Loan Assoc.

State of North Carolina
Executive Department

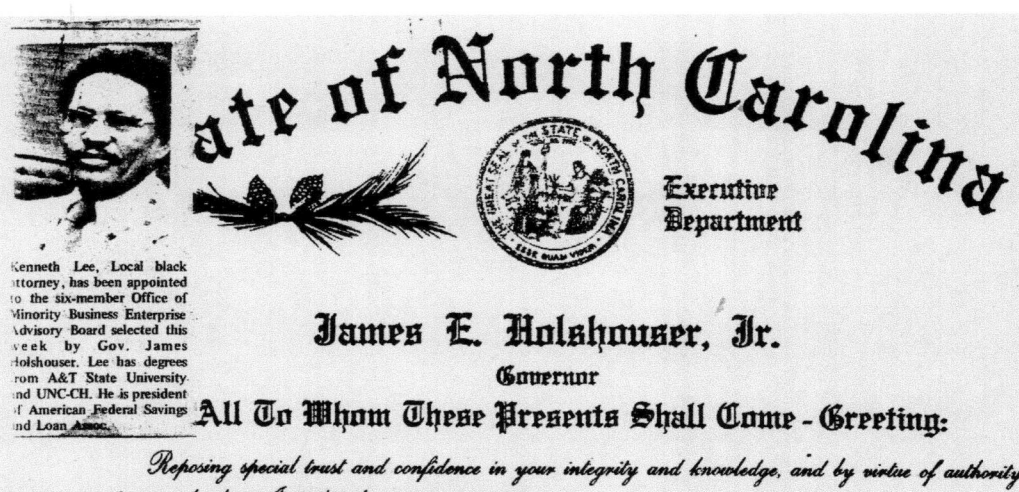

James E. Holshouser, Jr.
Governor

All To Whom These Presents Shall Come – Greeting:

Reposing special trust and confidence in your integrity and knowledge, and by virtue of authority vested in me by law, I do by these presents appoint J. KENNETH LEE as a member of the OFFICE OF MINORITY BUSINESS ENTERPRISE ADVISORY BOARD, to serve at the Pleasure of the Governor, and do hereby confer upon you all the rights, privileges and powers useful and necessary to the just and proper discharge of the duties of your appointment.

In Witness Whereof, I have hereunto signed my name and affixed the Great Seal of State, at the Capitol in the City of Raleigh, this twenty-seventh day of January in the year of our Lord one thousand nine hundred and seventy-six in the two hundredth year of our American Independence.

No Way!

[Page contains four certificate images rotated sideways, labeled Exhibit 12-21, 12-22, 12-23, and 12-24: United States Court of Appeals for the Fourth Circuit, Attorney General of the United States, Supreme Court of the United States, and Tax Court of the United States certificates for J. Kenneth Lee of North Carolina.]

Memories of Two Unforgettable Incidents

I can remember very vividly several specific incidents that have left their indelible stamps on me and that I have never been able to forget.

One such incident involved one of Papa's closest friends, Bro. C.T. Boyd who was pastor of the church in Chapel Hill. It took place at Papa's graveside (1947) just after he had been buried next to Mama and just when I was standing there alone, feeling that surely the whole world would now come to an end. In this setting, Bro. Boyd came over to me and placed his hand on my shoulder. "In a way son," he said, "you have been blessed to have had parents such as these, but in another way, you have been cursed."

Realizing my awe that he should say this, he continued: "You see, God only holds people responsible for their <u>conscious</u> wrongs, and no one is being accountable for his sins, unless he knows he has sinned. In your case, and because of the teaching and examples of your parents, you will be accountable for all of your wrongs." He may or may not have said something else before leaving, but this is all I remember. At times, the memory of this admonition has made everyday life awfully difficult.

One of my most interesting and unique experiences, I suppose, was the incident or series of incidents that led to my truce, or perhaps alliance, with the Ku Klux Klan. This story must be related in some detail.

Because of my involvement, as a participant and as a lawyer, in the Civil Rights Movement, the Klan had always harassed me. In addition to the calls and letters that I constantly received, I had had a bomb dropped in my front yard and the large plate glass window in the new office into which I had just moved had been broken out seven times in a period of just a few weeks in 1958. This rash of window breaking followed the initial integration of the public schools in Greensboro.

We had been successful in getting a student named Elijah Herring, Jr. enrolled in the Gillespie Park school in Greensboro, and because of this, the then Superintendent of School, Ben L. Smith, and the father of the child, Elijah Herring who ran a barber shop, had also been the subjects of some harassment and window breakings.

The story of my friendship and relationship with Elijah and with several other Blacks during this era, or at least the part that could be told, would make fascinating reading in itself. Suffice it to say here, however, that Elijah was a large, aggressive black man weighing about 250 pounds, who always carried a gun and who taught me the practical application of the doctrine of "self-help" that I had studied so long in law school. He feared no man and I cannot recall the number of times I had had to defend him in court on charges growing out of the use of his gun and other weapons in defense of the things he believed in. He died in the early 1960's of natural causes while I had a murder charge against him pending on appeal in the Supreme Court.

As a prerequisite to survival, I had an unusual friendship and rapport with Elijah and several other Blacks who shared his philosophy. Whenever we had a new case filed to integrate a new facility such as a swimming pool, golf course, school etc., the rash of harassments would immediately follow. These friends, usually organized by Elijah, without my request but most times with my knowledge, would arm and secrete themselves around my house and provide protection for my family and me until the immediate danger had passed. These friends, who were generally regarded by the "powers that be" as the criminal element in the black community, were regarded by me as some of the most dedicated participants in the Civil Rights Movement because they did very little talking but were always willing to risk their lives as "back stops" to others who were out front in the movement. We shared a tremendous amount of mutual respect.

When the police could not or would not do anything about the series of glass breaking at my office, Elijah and company took over. After the sixth breaking, they organized and secreted themselves all around the area in cars and on foot to wait for the next occurrence. What happened after that, or on the seventh breaking, is a matter of public record.

A car came by being driven by a 17-year-old boy and occupied by a 28-year-old Klansman named Clyde Webster. As they passed my office, Webster threw a bottle through the window. Perhaps the most sensible decision that Clyde Webster ever made was not to resist when Elijah and the other Blacks closed in on him and stopped the car. The case received a large amount of publicity and eventually came up for trial in the District Court. Webster was given an active jail sentence that he appealed and the 17 year old was given a suspended sentence. As it came out during the trial and resulting investigations, Webster was a very prominent figure, state officer and leader in the Klan.

When this occurred in late 1958, I had stopped taking new civil rights cases, was in the process of completing those I had pending and was just starting to build my new house.

You can imagine my surprise and other feelings when one day, shortly after Webster was convicted, I looked up to see him standing immediately in front of my desk and looking down at me. I had never spoken to him, had only seen him in court and had no idea why he would be there except to retaliate for the active jail sentence he had just gotten because of me. Instinctively, I shifted my body toward the right drawer of my desk where, at that time, I always kept a gun. I think he sensed this and immediately relieved the tension by announcing that he had come to talk to me about something unrelated to the incident that caused his conviction. I asked him to sit down and he began to tell me about his reason for coming.

To abbreviate this story as much as possible, it seemed that he was a carpenter and, I believe, the superintendent for the contractor I had engaged to help build my house. He related a series of incidents that had happened to him since his arrest and the resulting publicity for breaking the windows.

He never apologized for his views, although he did apologize for his action toward me, and advised me that his employer had told him that he was no longer employed. The only job he had at the time was my house and he could no longer work there.

From the time he walked in, he addressed me as "Mr. Lee." a title he used from that time until the last time I talked with him. I cannot remember verbatim the conversation we had in the office, but in essence, this is what he said to me. "Mr. Lee, I don't have anything against you personally. I don't even know you, except that you're a symbol of one thing and I'm a symbol of another. I ain't never going to promise you that I'll change my feeling about segregation, but I will promise you that I won't do anything else to hurt you personally. I've got a family to support and I need my job. If you won't object to me working on your house, I'll do the best job I know how to do and I'm a damn good carpenter and you don't ever have to speak to me if you don't want to."

Well this was the most unique approach to solving a problem I had ever encountered and, while he still had me in a trance, I agreed not to object to his working on the job.

What happened after that was indeed an experience. Construction on my house began; it lasted approximately 7 or 8 months. All of the other workmen on the job called Clyde "Hammer" which I later learned was a nickname that he earned because of his exceptional ability as a carpenter. We gradually got to know each other better, and as the job progressed, he would often call or contact me with suggestions as to how the architect's plan or what the contractor was doing could be altered to either give me a better structure or save me money without compromising the quality of the building. When I would check this out with the architect or builder, invariably they would agree and wonder how I came to know so much about building. Eventually, Clyde and I got to the place where we joked and laughed constantly about the differences between our philosophies. My bedroom wall facing the street has a large sliding glass door and window that cover the full wall on that side of the room. I recall one day when I was there and Clyde had just finished framing the wall for the glass doors and window, he stepped back, looked at it and said: "Yeah, that's big enough for me to hit with a bottle from the street." We both had a big laugh and thought nothing else about it.

When his trial came up on appeal in Superior Court, he was again convicted. The house, however, had been completed and just prior to the time the Judge was to sentence him, his lawyer subpoenaed me and asked me about the events that had occurred between "Hammer" and me since the last trial. I related the events just as they had happened and, afterwards, the Judge gave him a suspended sentence. The courtroom was filled with his Klan friends and immediately after the trial, he approached me in the hall with several of the top Klan officials. He reached out to shake my hand and said: "Mr. Lee, I appreciate everything you did, and I just want to let you know that if anybody in this town ever messes with you, all you got to do is call us."

Lee's New Home Built With "Hammer-The Klansman" as Lead Carpenter for Framing Contractor

I always felt that this must have been some kind of "unholy alliance," but from that day to this, I have not been harassed or received any of the phone calls that I had contended with prior to that time.

A few weeks later when school opened for the 1959-60 school year, Elijah Herring, Jr. was in attendance at Gillespie Park School and the white pickets were still trying to discourage it. I rode by the school one day and there was Hammer leading the line of pickets with a sign that must have been at least 4 feet square saying "NIGGER GO HOME." He looked toward the street, saw me passing, threw up his hand and hollered as loud as he could, "Hey, Mr. Lee, how you been doing?"

Hammer died a few months ago without ever compromising his beliefs. Although it had to be a "bastard" type friendship, I still regarded him a friend from the day he left my office until the day he died.

Sarah Lownes Lee, Mama, in Old Car with Her
Constant Companion, Son Ken in the 1930s

[Photos of the family ended his Chapter in *Offshoots: The H. F. Lee Family Book*] Other images replace them in his Memoirs.

Ken's Tribute (and Confession) to Mama and Papa

Just before the back cover was placed on The H.F. Lee Family Book in 1979, somebody [probably some family member who had not put in long days of preparation of the massive tome] came up with the bright idea that we should all write tributes to Mama and Papa. The one written by Ken turned into a confession.

TO MAMA AND PAPA

It must have been apparent to all the other children in the family that there was always something special in my love and attachment to Mama. Looking back on this relationship now, I know in many ways it was Papa's great love for her that inspired me to emulate his relationship with her. Mama was always so self-sacrificing for the rest of us and always so careful not to call attention to this fact. Papa was the one in the limelight, the head of the family in every sense of the word. If you ever slipped up and forgot that fact, Papa had ways of reminding you. I remember once, when I was a pre-schooler, riding into town with Papa and Mama and waiting in the car with Papa while Mama ran in the store to pick up a package.

When 15 minutes passed and Mama had failed to emerge from the store, Papa mumbled out a few general complaints about women shoppers. As the minutes continued to tick by his mumbling became more specific and articulate, and I decided I could agree with him and express a complaint about Mama's slowness. No sooner than I had gotten the first words out of my mouth did I realize what a mistake I had made. Mama was to be criticized by no small up-start of a son! Not Papa's wife! You can bet I never made that mistake again. Neither did my brief moment of fault finding with Mama affect my real ambition to give her all the things I thought she deserved from life.

Looking back now on all the factors that push me toward achieving most of my life's ambitions, I realize how much the combined influence of these two wonderful parents had on me in the formative years of my life. My greatest regret is that Mama never lived long enough to collect her rewards from me; and Papa, without Mama, was around only long enough to be sure their early efforts were not totally in vain.

Ken

No Way!

VISITORS PASS REQUEST
10ND-NavBase-Gtmo-1408

NAVBASEGTMOINST 5651.1
NB37:002:IRA:rrk

UNITED STATES NAVAL BASE
GUANTANAMO BAY, CUBA

DATE 12 OCTOBER 1969

From: MICHAEL E. LEE AC2 6953887 USN NAS/AAWC
TO: COMMANDER NAVAL BASE

It is requested that permission be granted to bring the following visitor(s) on the Naval Base.

Name	Age	Sex	No. of Days	Inclusive Dates
J. KENNETH LEE	41	M	7	30 OCT.'69-07 NOV.'69
NANCY Y. LEE	39	F	7	SAME AS ABOVE

The following information is furnished in connection with above

A. ☒ VISITOR'S PASS: (For social visit only—limit 30 days).
Visitor's Nationality: USA
Reason for Visit: SOCIAL VISIT WITH FAMILY

B. ☐ ENTRY PERMIT: For purpose of establishing residence legal authority for checkage of quarters allowance.
C. QUARTERS TO BE OCCUPIED DH311 Number
D. POINT OF ENTRY: Main Gate ☐ Northeast Gate ☐

I am acquainted with all rules and regulations as pertaining to visitors on this Base and will comply with them strictly.

(1) _Michael E. Lee_
Signature of Applicant

(2) RECOMMENDED APPROVAL _____
CO of Command Concerned

(3) CLEARANCE CHECK (except on U.S. Citizens) _____
Base Provost Marshal

(4) APPROVED/DISAPPROVED: _Clarke by direction_
Commander Naval Base, Guantanamo Bay, Cuba

Enclosure (1)

The Lees Visit to Guantanamo Bay, Cuba when Michael (in Navy) and Wife, Sandra, Became Parents of First Grandchild, Kenney, 1959

Card Lee Kept Among Memorabilia from WWII; He Can't Remember Why

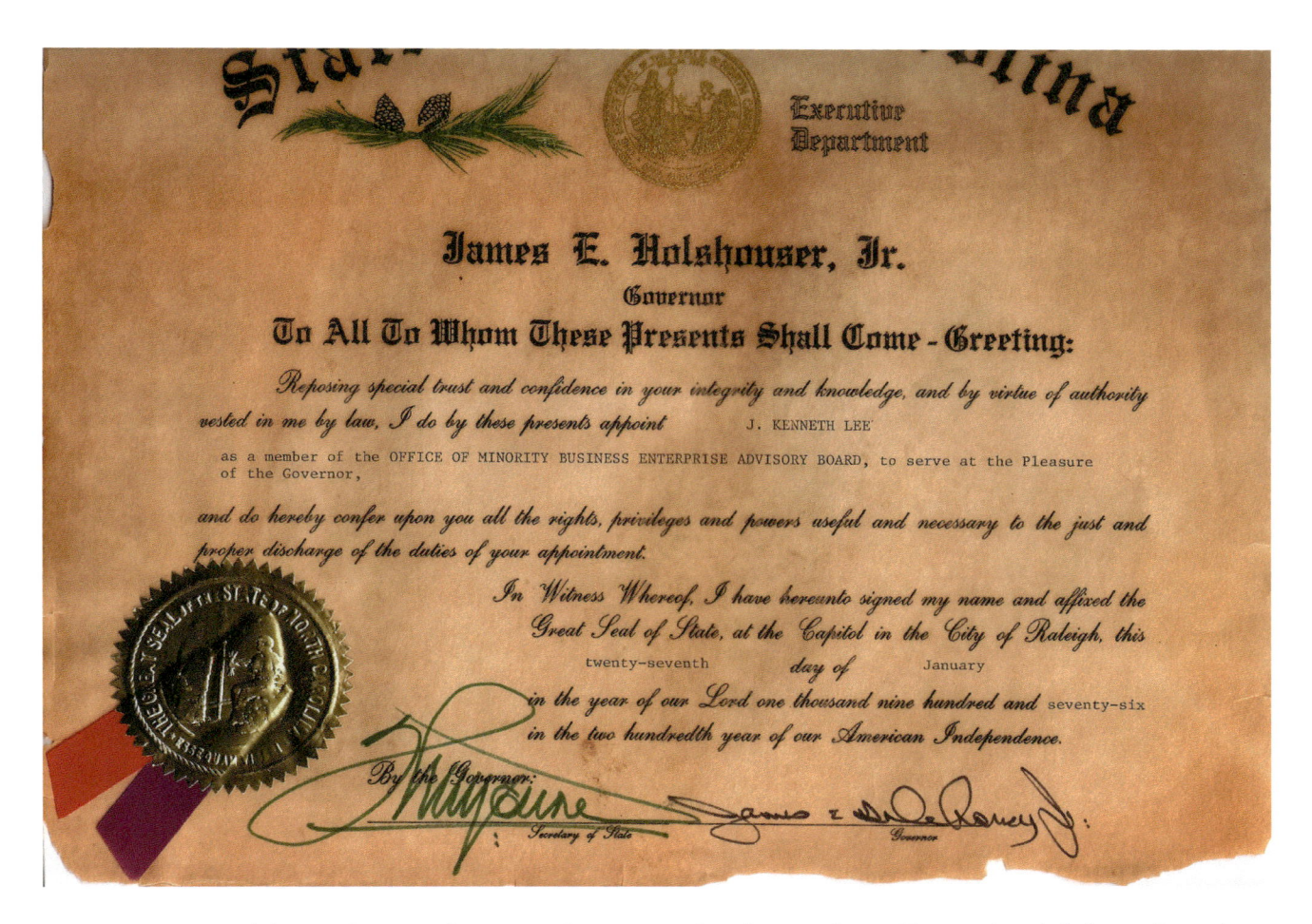

Governor Halshauser's Appointment of Ken to Minority Business Enterprise Advisory Board

Kenneth Lee is presented the award of the Order of the Long Leaf Pine by Alexander Killens, Assistant to the Governor of North Carolina.

Lee Accepts the State's Highest Honor, the Long Leaf Pine Award from the Governor

Lee Family at Reception in Michaels' Home for Governor Martin.
From L to R: Michael, Nancy, Governor Martin, Sandra, Kenneth

CITY OF GREENSBORO
NORTH CAROLINA

March 6, 1970

CITY COUNCIL

Dear Nancy and Kenneth:

    Please forgive me for being so tardy in writing but a trip out of town has thrown me behind schedule. I sincerely want to thank you for the warm hospitality you afforded us weekend before last. It was awfully nice of you to let an army track through your beautiful home, but I think this visit was most important in our trip around the city. Even though there are a lot of problems in our city, it's still a pretty great place to live.

    Thanks again for your hospitality.

Sincerely yours,

Jim Melvin

Mr. and Mrs. J. Kenneth Lee
1021 Broad Avenue
Greensboro, North Carolina

Letter of Appreciation to Lees for Permitting Bus
Load of Visitors to View Their New Home, Greensboro

A LETTER FROM THE PRESIDENT

Dear Prospective Member:

For many years we have all dreamed of someday having the opportunity of belonging to a first class COUNTRY CLUB with all of the privileges and opportunities such membership affords. Now that dream can become a reality and you have the opportunity of becoming a charter member of the finest and perhaps the only club of its kind in the Nation, owned and operated solely by Negroes.

The FOREST LAKE COUNTRY CLUB, INC. was officially chartered by the State of North Carolina on the 14th day of September, 1959, and on Nov. 2, 1959, the Corporation purchased from Burlington Industries, a 124 acre tract of land, together with all buildings and furnishings, formerly used by them as a country club.

The FOREST LAKE COUNTRY CLUB, INC. is not a NIGHT CLUB although it contains a clubhouse with facilities for dining, dancing and entertainment that exceeds anything that you have perhaps ever experienced. Its primary purpose is a facility that can be used and enjoyed by the entire family, from the youngest to the oldest, and this brochure is presented for the purpose of introducing you to some of these facilities.

We are convinced that there is a definite demand for such facilities as this club has to offer. You cannot become a member of the club unless you are also a part owner and we sincerely hope that you will join with us in perpetuating the idea which we have advanced and make your club a credit to your community and a source of enjoyment and happiness to you, your family and friends.

On behalf of the officers and directors, I extend to you our sincere invitation to inspect these facilities and submit your application for membership if you so desire.

Very Truly Yours
J. Kenneth Lee, President

President Kenneth Lee's Invitation To New Country Club For Blacks in Greensboro

Lees Attending Grandson Mike's High School Graduation Ceremony

PAGE B2

THE CAMERA'S EYE

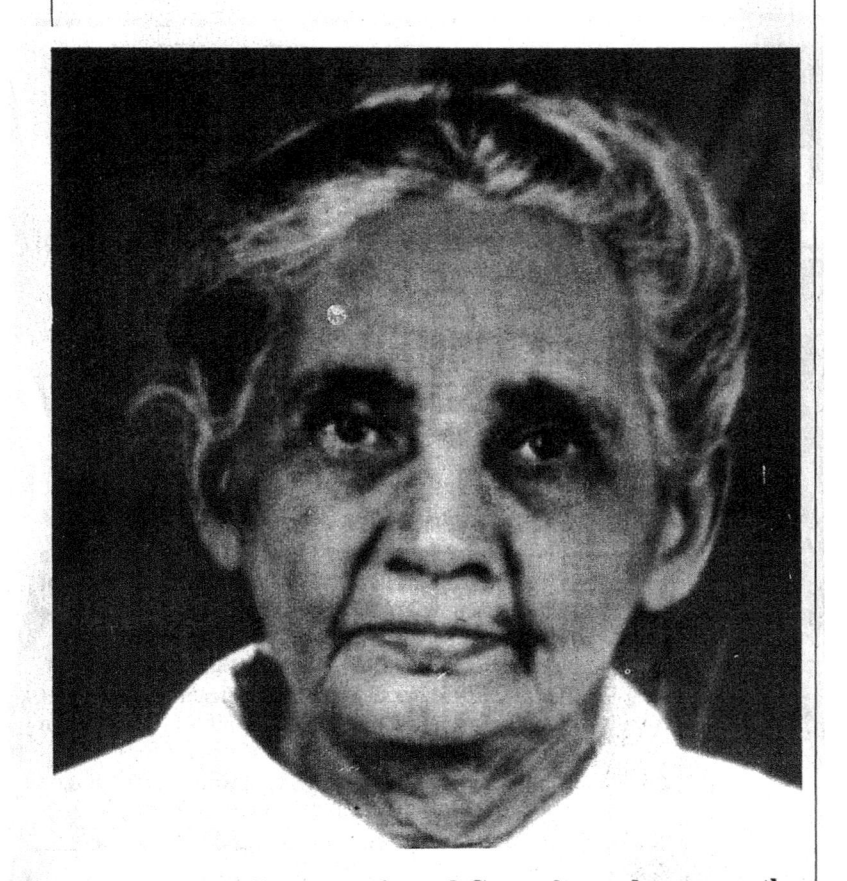

The Lincoln Grove section of Greensboro, known as the Big Road Community before 1914, was home to a number of Greensboro's first African-American families, including the Lees, Graves, McAdoos, and Dansbys. Shown here are former slave Martha Bigelow Lee, grandmother of American Federal's J. Kenneth Lee. (see Section C) and Mr. and Mrs. John Graves, parents of Rev. Prince Graves (See Page A1). Readers who wish to submit old photographs of early African-American Greensboro places, people, and events for publication in the Peacemaker, should contact Joe Daniels at 274-6210.

Courtesy of *CAROLINA PEACEMAKER*,
Saturday, June 17, 1989, p. B2
Greensboro, North Carolina

Grandma Martha Lee in Spotlight News Article for Lincoln Grove Development

At first, the rural community was called "Big Road" after the dusty road which connected it to the little town of Greensboro of fewer than 10,000 residents.

After 1914, it began to be called "Lincoln Grove," and eventually it became part of Greensboro as the city expanded.

In 1985 the Lincoln Grove community became the home of the Lincoln Grove Shopping Center.

From Plan to Reality

The echoes and shadows of enterprising pioneer families punctuate this account of Lincoln Grove's development since the closing years of the Nineteenth Century.

From the time that Lincoln Grove was the Big Road Community, its story has been one of people living and working together through changing, often difficult times. The ups and downs and ups of "The Grove" (as it came to be affectionately and sometimes not-so-affectionately known) mark the community's journey from Big Road, culminating in the the completion of the Lincoln Grove Shopping Center in the Spring of 1985.

This report of the Lincoln Grove Corporation describes its shopping center undertaking from plan to reality — a year of successful private sector effort in partnership with government and the community.

Lincoln Grove Corporation hopes that this report, **Journey from Big Road,** helps to put into perspective the creative energy which had its roots in Lincoln Grove's years of struggle and enterprise, in the unique economic and human needs of a unique community. The shopping center is a living memorial to that tradition of human excellence, and we hope that this report reflects the faith in and love for the community, and faith in the future of Greensboro, which the shopping center represents.

J. Kenneth Lee
President

Enterprise Spirit

President Ronald Reagan in his 1985 inaugural address stated: "The time has come for a new American emancipation, a great national drive to tear down economic barriers and liberate the spirit of enterprise in the most distressed areas of the country." The UDAG commitment to Lincoln Grove is a reflection of "the spirit of enterprise" of which the President spoke.

In announcing the Lincoln Grove Shopping Center UDAG grant, Secretary Samuel Pierce of the Department stressed the role of partnerships between public and private sectors in fostering such economic development activity for areas such as Lincoln Grove/Greensboro.

Journey from Big Road
©1985 by Lincoln Grove Corporation

The 20,000-square-foot Lincoln Grove Shopping Center is owned by the Lincoln Grove Corporation, a minority firm of which J. Kenneth Lee is president and the Reverend Prince E. Graves, Melvin T. Alexander, and Gladys Minor are other principals.

Lincoln Grove Report, p.1 Submitted by Pres. Lee for Greensboro Community Development Project—The Conversion of the Big Road Community into Lincoln Grove.

The National Recognition Program for Community Development Excellence

of the

U.S. Department of Housing and Urban Development

presents this

Certificate of National Recognition

to the participants in the

LINCOLN GROVE SHOPPING CENTER

GREENSBORO, NORTH CAROLINA

For your contribution to fostering public/private partnerships for the greater benefit of your community.

Samuel R. Pierce, Jr.
Secretary,
U.S. Department of Housing and Urban Development
1986

Certificate of National Recognition for Lincoln Grove Leadership Group for Lincoln Grove

in Morningside, we're family people who want a good environment for our families. Something had to give. Something had to happen. And it's happening. . . for the better as I see it. Dreams can pay off."

The Lincoln Grove Shopping Center story is the story of three men and one woman who skillfully developed the plans and engineered the financing and construction of a shopping center: J. Kenneth Lee, the Reverend Prince Graves, Gladys Minor, and Melvin Alexander, the officers of the Lincoln Grove Corporation.

It is the story of the Corporation's efforts, the faith of two black-owned financial institutions, the teamwork of hundreds of Lincoln Grove residents, the support of local, state, and federal government agen-

Place Called Home

Lincoln Grove had become just a crowded neighborhood of houses. The new center is making the houses seem more like home, and you know everyone of God's children ought to have a place they can call home.

Leadership for Progress

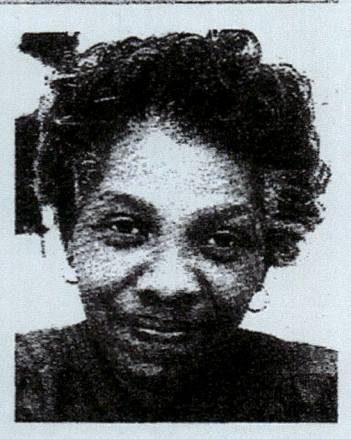

Organizers

Graves (top left), Alexander (bottom left), Lee (center), and Minor (right) — spearheaders of the shopping center development.

Building Tributes to Nancy and Mama Lee:
Top Photo: Nancy Lee Fellowship Hall, New Beginning Community Outreach Church
Lower: Sarah Lee Fitness Center at YMCA, Market St., Greensboro

Lee's Sister, Winona, with Family, Daughter Betty and Granddaughter Olivia on a Visit to Grandma Lee's Portrait in YMCA Lobby. Four Generations

The Barristers (wives of lawyers) with Ken and Nan in
Appreciation of Scholarship Donated in Nan's Name

BENNETT COLLEGE
Greensboro, North Carolina 27420

DEPARTMENT OF BUSINESS
AND ECONOMICS

(919) 273-4431
EXT. 128

March 3, 1987

Attorney and Mrs. Kenneth Lee
1021 Broad Avenue
Greensboro, NC 27406

Dear Attorney and Mrs. Lee:

Thank you for your generous gift of $22,000 to make the home of President and Mrs. Jones an alumnae house.

Alumnae enjoy visiting the College to view the campus, and you have given them another great reason to visit their alma mater.

We thank you for sharing your success with the college family. Again, thank you, Attorney and Mrs. Lee.

Sincerely yours,

Thelma Baker
Cynthia Bridgett
Marquerette Byrd
Constance Lindsey
Latosaka Stephens
Tonya Zarate

Generous donors Nancy and Kenneth Lee

Letter of Appreciation for Gift to Bennett College in Nan's Honor

No Way!

Photo of Inductees

PROGRAM

National Bar Association ❧ Annual Awards Banquet
Friday, July 31, 1992

Robin Smith, News Anchor
KMOV-TV, Channel 4
St. Louis, Missouri
Presiding

Procession of Dais Guests	Introductions by Robin Smith
Invocation	Rev. Emery Washington, Sr. All Saints Episcopal Church, St. Louis, Missouri
Musical Selection	Anita Watkins-Stevens, St. Louis, Missouri
Dinner	
Introduction of Speaker	Star Jones, Legal Correspondent NBC News, New York, New York
Banquet Address	Honorable Bill Clinton Democratic Candidate for President of the United States, Little Rock, Arkansas
Recognition of the National Bar Association "Hall of Fame" Inductees	Benjamin J. Pigott, Chair NBA Lawyers "Hall of Fame" Task Force, Houston, Texas
Introduction of President 1991-1992	Mark McPhail Roger McPhail
Presentation of C. Francis Stradford, Equal Justice and Special Awards	Sharon McPhail, President National Bar Association, Detroit, Michigan
President's Epilogue 1991-1992	Sharon McPhail, Esquire
Presentation	Darwyn P. Fair, President Wolverine Bar Association, Detroit, Michigan
Installation of NBA Officers 1992-1993	
Installation of President 1992-1993	Honorable Marion J. Johnson, Judge, Los Angeles Municipal Court, Los Angeles, California
Introduction of President	Wallace L. Walker, Esquire Philadelphia, Pennsylvania
Remarks by the President	Allen J. Webster, Jr., Esquire Inglewood, California
Benediction	Reverend Emery Washington, Sr.

Banquet Program from Hall of Fame with Honorable Bill Clinton
as Speaker Before He Became President, 1992

No Way!

THE North Carolina State Bar

Awards this Certificate of Appreciation to

J. Kenneth Lee

In recognition of the completion of

Fifty Years Or More Of Service

as a member of The North Carolina State Bar.

By Order of the Council of the North Carolina State Bar.
Presented this 17th day of October, 2002.

UNC Law School Certificate of Appreciation for 50 Years of Service

NORTH CAROLINA AGRICULTURAL AND TECHNICAL STATE UNIVERSITY
GREENSBORO
27411
(919) 379-7940

EDWARD B. FORT
Chancellor

April 19, 1984

Attorney J. Kenneth Lee
3011 East Market Street
Greensboro, North Carolina   27406

Dear Attorney Lee:

It is my great pleasure to inform you that the Board of Trustees, in its regular meeting on April 18, 1984, voted unanimously to bestow upon you the Honorary Degree of DOCTOR OF LAWS, to be conferred at our 1984 Commencement on May 6, 1984, at 11:00 a.m., at the Greensboro Coliseum on West Lee Street. We sincerely hope that your schedule will allow you to be present to receive this award.

Because this honor will be bestowed at this prestigious occasion, you are included in the platform arrangement as a member of the Chancellor's Party, all of whom will be adorned in academic attire. Members of the Chancellor's Party will assemble in the Town Hall of the Coliseum Complex at 10:00 a.m. for robing and preparation for the academic procession. We will provide academic attire for you and have it available in the Town Hall.

Should Mrs. Lee accompany you, she will be seated in a special reserved section for spouses of our program participants and special guests. She may report with you to the Town Hall and then be escorted to that special area.

Immediately following the commencement program, we invite you and Mrs. Lee to join the speaker, members of the Board of Trustees and other special platform guests in the receiving line at the reception for graduating classes, alumni and friends for one hour--from 1:00 to 2:00 p.m.

Following the reception, Mrs. Fort and I would be honored to have you and Mrs. Lee join us for dinner on the campus. Dinner will be served in The commons area of Williams Cafeteria at approximately 2:30 p.m., the time we estimate it will take to get to the campus from the Coliseum.

We hope that you will be able to be present for this occasion. Your immediate response will be appreciated.

Sincerely,

Edward B. Fort
Chancellor

An Equal Opportunity / Affirmative Action Employer
A Constituent Institution of THE UNIVERSITY OF NORTH CAROLINA

NCA&T Awarding of Honorary Doctor's Degree to Lee

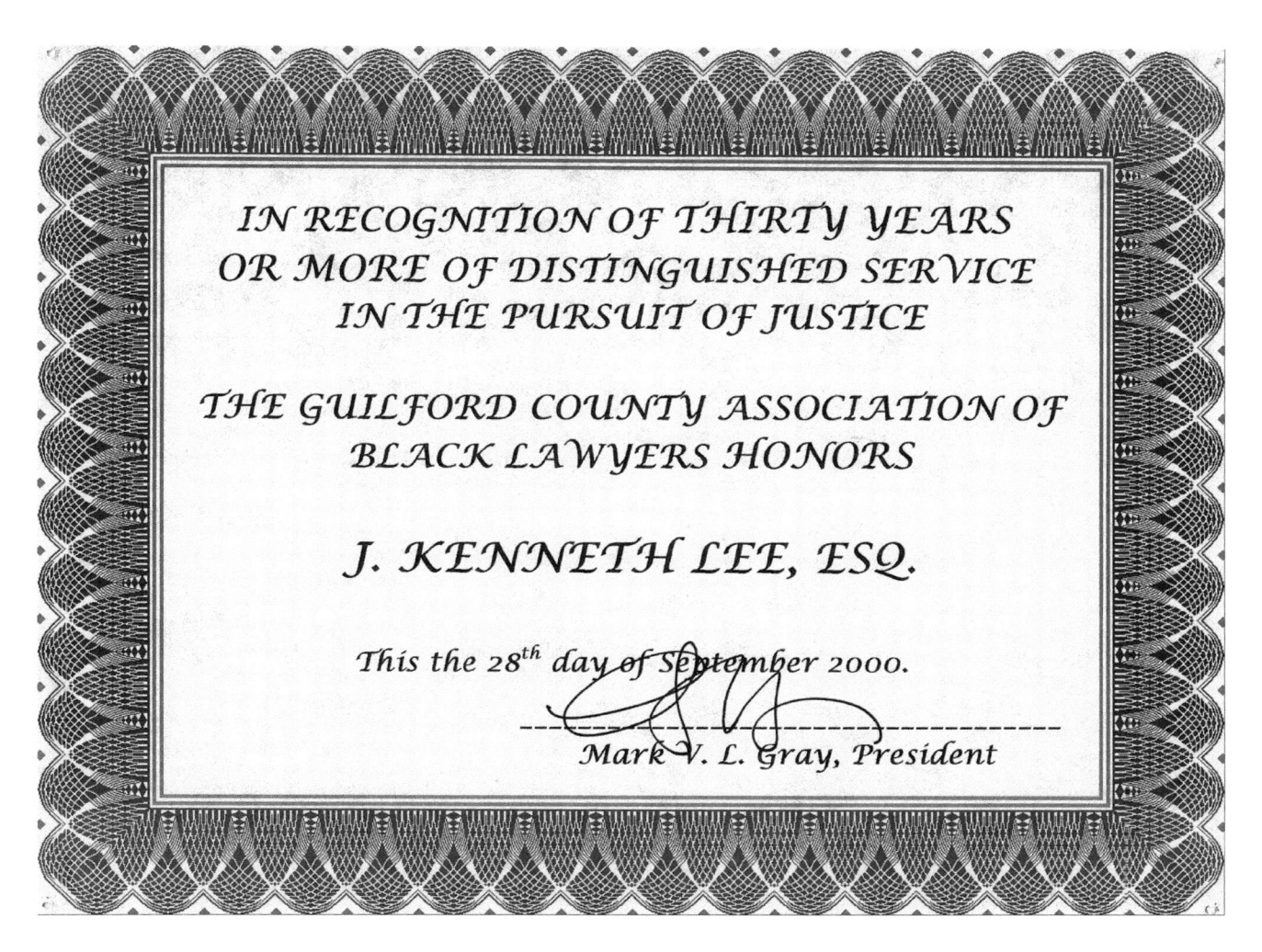

> IN RECOGNITION OF THIRTY YEARS
> OR MORE OF DISTINGUISHED SERVICE
> IN THE PURSUIT OF JUSTICE
>
> THE GUILFORD COUNTY ASSOCIATION OF
> BLACK LAWYERS HONORS
>
> **J. KENNETH LEE, ESQ.**
>
> This the 28th day of September 2000.
>
> Mark V. L. Gray, President

Black Lawyers Certificate to Lee for 30 Years of Service

Golden Rams

During the 2007 Black Alumni Reunion, the Golden Rams Society was born. There was the belief that those African-American students who earned a degree from the University of North Carolina should be inducted into the Society on the 50th anniversary of their graduation. As these inductions are to be an annual event at future Black Alumni Reunions, we salute the first inductees whose name, degree earned and year of graduation are introduced below.

Harvey E. Beech '52 (LLB)*

J. Kenneth Lee '52 (LLBJD)

James Robert Walker '52 (LLB)*

Major Stonington High '53 (LLBJD)*

Edward Oscar Diggs '55 (MD)

Donald Bernard Horton '65 (MA)

Romallus Olga Murphy '56 (LLBJD)

George Royster Greene '57 (LLBJD)

Daniel Lanier '57 (MSW)

James Norfleet Slade '57 (MD)*

UNC Black Lawyers Induction into Black Rams in 2007

Voice of a Young Son—Michael

Editors Note: Just as this manuscript was about to come together [finally] as a collection of diverse opinions about one man, a package arrived from the man himself with a note that read: "Found this booklet in the bottom of a drawer downstairs. Mike made it for Father's Day when he was quite young. Not significant. Just thought you might enjoy looking at it."

Ken is so wrong about this discovery, or the booklet, being insignificant. To me it is Mike's way of being sure his voice from the great beyond is a part of his Dad's book. [Michael, who followed in his father's footsteps to become a successful lawyer, died unexpectedly at age 49.]

He had bound news articles, certificates etc, into a folder with two loving notes. The note at the beginning of the collection read:

Dear Dad,
    Hope your Father's Day was a pleasant
one. Mom and me sure have tried hard to make
it a Father's Day worthy of any good father like
you.
    Seldom do we realize how lucky we are.
It is my earnest hope that we will spend many
other Father's Days together.
                                                                Mike

The note at the end of the collection read:

Dear Dad.
    These are only a few of the things that you
have done. You fight for what you believe in, and
in doing this you have done many things for your
race and for your people.
Of this we are proud. Of you most of all.
Happy Father's Day Dad.
                                                                Mike

[Mike later became one of the many students that his Father had to get released from jail during the early sit-in movement in Greensboro.]

I'm beginning to believe in miracles. The day before receiving Ken's package, I had found a letter written by him to Sister Lil when we were working on The Family Book in 1976 [included here]; it not only mentions Mike's collection, but reveals much about Ken as a brother.

Two other things from Mike's collection enforced my belief in miracles: 1) a photo from Ken's collection of the men who brought the suit against UNC in 1951. [Included here]; and 2) articles with headlines that have now given me access to many of the news stories that remained undocumented or unapproved for reprinting in this Book. Because the headlines tell a story of their own, a sample of them is given here. [Thanks Mike--you're in.]

NEWS HEADLINES

First at University of North Carolina in 162 Years
Federal Judge Bars Negro Law Students from University of North Carolina: Rules Their Facilities Equal
Law School Appeal To Be Heard Soon
Dorm Segregation Problem Raised
Five Negroes Send Telegram to Governor Scott
First Negro Law Student of Chapel Hill Admitted to Bar Here
Brilliant Negro Lawyer: Atty. J. Kenneth Lee
Cumberland Professional Building Rising on Pearson Street
Local Negro Will Seek UNC Quarters Today
Negro Seeks Dorm Room
Golf Case Arguments Slated
Negro Lawyer Is Candidate for Counsel
Placement in Schools Is Held Up: Negro Attorney Protests Action
Kenneth Lee, '44, Spearheads Group to Construct Million Dollar Center
He Thinks, Plans Big
Old Hospital Renovation Begins; Nursing Facility Planned
Some People for Progress: J. Kenneth Lee
Group Plans Meeting on Segregation
Local Attorney in $3 Million Apartment Deal
3 Bankers Remain on State Agency
Klansman Sentenced to Roads
2 Arrested in Breaking of Windows
They Must Be Twice As Good [Article written by Michael]

J. KENNETH LEE
ATTORNEY AT LAW
P. O. BOX 20027
GREENSBORO, N. C. 27420

OFFICES
107 NORTH MURROW BLVD.

February 16, 1976

TELEPHONE
(919) 274-3749

Mrs. Lillian L. Humphrey
1653 Lawrence Circle Drive
Daytona Beach, Florida   32017

Dear Lil:

I received your latest letter and have already mailed the letters which you sent to the proper people. You should be hearing from them shortly.

I have been too trifling or lazy to compile the information which you requested. However, I think you made a serious mistake when you said in your letter that if I could send you some material, perhaps you or Wy could compile it. That was the excuse I had been looking for.

A little while back, on Father's Day, Mike compiled a book of old clippings and stuff which he and Nancy dug up from somewhere and gave it to me for Father's Day. I have added a few things and am sending the whole shebang to you. I hate to put you through this, but maybe you can find something that will be of some value when you start writing. Wy used to write all of my speeches for me, so actually, the only reason I am sending the material in this form, is because I know it will be done much better if its done by you or Wy. Its not that I'm too lazy to do it myself like you think.

I really had planned to make a very significant contribution to your book, but it is beginning to look now like that will fall through. When I was on crutches and had lots of time on my hands, I went over to the Caswell County Court House in Yanceyville to search some old records relating to another matter. While there, and solely by accident, I stumbled across a lead to some records involving our family tree. I even ran across one document, which I felt showed pretty conclusively that one of your ancestors was traded for a mule.

I had copies made of these documents and apparently hid them

Mrs. Lillian L. Humphrey
Page 2
February 16, 1976

from myself, since I looked all weekend and could not find them. Record keeping was very shoddy in those days, especially where Negroes were concerned, since they were considered chattels. Consequently, you cannot re-locate such records by searching name indexes, etc. as is normally done. I came across these by checking some conveyances made by a white family whose name I cannot now recall. I will, however, before you get ready to publish, go over and check again to see if I can get lucky. Don't depend on it though.

I am not certain of the trip to Florida. We were going to attend a group meeting in Orlando, but the meeting is set for the same dates as both the C. I. A. A. and the M. E. A C. basketball tournaments here and in Norfolk. Consequently, most of the group has switched plans. If I do go, however, I'll be by to see you.

I am enclosing some stamps and some change to help you out with expenses of mailing paper, etc. When you get ready to put it in final form, let me know. I'll take care of the printing.

Love to Polly and Henry and maybe I'll get to see all of you on the weekend about February 27th.

Sincerely,

Kenneth

JKL:ghm

Enclosure

Part II
Lee Through The Voices of Others And Selected Memorabilia

Since Sister Lillian's words of love from the Lee Family Book motivated the current endeavor on J. Kenneth Lee, it seems appropriate that a maxim from the family book should take us into Part II where we examine what others believe Lee to be.

It has been said that one is three persons:
the person he thinks he is (his ego), the person
he really is (his character), and the person others
believe him to be (his reputation.)

As "the Book" was nearing completion in 1979 [by now the readers should know that I have found a sneaky way to get much of both books before the public], Lil and I as co-editors decided that a true picture of the family would not be possible without permitting the voices of our friends to be heard. Thus, we sent out letters inviting friends to share testimonies of their friendship with one or more members of the family, assuring them that one's reputation is not in his or her own keeping but at the mercy of others. We urged them to be candid, individualistic and brief in their responses and ended the letter with the following anonymous poem. [We are good at using the wisdom of others to enforce our thoughts!]

OUR FRIENDS ARE PART OF WHO WE ARE

> The happiest business in the world
> Is that of making friends;
> And no investment on the 'street'
> Pays larger dividends.
> For life is more than stocks and bonds;
> And love, than rate per cent;
> And he who gives in friendship's name
> Shall reap as he has spent.
> Life is the greatest investment,
> And no man lives in vain

> Who guards a hundred friendships
> As a miser guards his gain.

The response from friends was overwhelming [though seldom brief]. Selected responses recorded for Ken between March, 1974 and December, 1977 become a significant part of the voices heard from those shared in this part of the present volume—but first things first.

Voices of Close Kin: Those who knew him "WHEN"

Kenneth was born in Charlotte, North Carolina, in 1923, the last child born before Papa moved his family to Hamlet. Ken was a mere toddler when the "Rev. Papa Lee" found a small Church of God following there and decided it was a good place to raise a family. [The large family also increased the size of his congregation as we spent a lot of time in church.]

We lived, literally, by the side of the road between Hamlet and Rockingham in a house built by Papa, the older boys, and any volunteers Papa could recruit. [In later years, Ken tried, unsuccessfully, to purchase the property in Hamlet for sentimental reasons.] Most of the time there were no more than seven children living in the house at one time. Kenny, as the siblings called him [when they weren't calling him other names], established early that Mama "belonged to him," thus, securing his place as the center of attention in the house [and elsewhere]. No place is this memory of Baby Brother made clearer than in the individual chapters of The H.F. Lee Family Book. Ken was always just below the surface of everybody's memory.

House By the Side of the Road: Family Home in Hamlet, NC,
Built by Papa, Sons and Volunteers in Mid 1920s

No Way!

Alvis, was the little "Big Brother" in the "big open sedan" [Ken thinks it may have been the Essex] that provided transportation for the family from Charlotte to the "side of the road" house in Hamlet; he recalls one of his favorite stories of Ken. [Ken was safely tucked into Mama's lap in the front seat; no seatbelts to worry about!] Apparently the short 80 miles trip was prolonged by many side of the road stops to change a flat tire on the old car. Shortly after one such stop, a loud backfire from a passing car startled Ken evoking a loud "Oh, oh, another puncture!" from him. [Even then, he never missed a thing!]

One of Lil's unforgettable memories reflects the hardships endured by the family during the 1930's Great Depression [and the love that the family found to endure them]. Papa had sadly and reluctantly interrupted Lil's early college days in Greensboro when he could no longer spare the $1.00 a week he paid a relative for her room and board. [Not very long after being called home, she obtained a scholarship and returned to college.] She had begun writing a postal card that was never sent to a friend. Ken found the card and informed her that the card had to be used "since we can't afford to waste a penny post card!" [He learned early the value of a penny as we all found out later. It should be noted here that Papa expressed a fierce determination that all of his girls get a college education to keep them out of somebody else's kitchen. Luckily, Ken, being born in the midst of a flurry of girls, got in on that deal.]

Bess gave the title "But for the Grace of God" to her favorite memory of Ken when she repeated it at family gatherings [and any where else she could find a listener]. Bess was the older sister who claimed that she became one-sided from carrying Baby Ken around on her right hip. This story, however, was about Ken-the-World-War II Vet. It seems that Ken was just released from service in the Pacific at the end of the War. He had stopped off in Detroit, invited Bess and Polly to accompany him to NC in a used car he purchased in Detroit [the operative word is USED]. Ken was in the front seat, Polly in the back--sleeping-- while Bess was driving through the worst mountains in West Virginia. Ken suddenly had a nightmare [probably thought he was still fighting the enemy], started clutching at the windshield, then the steering wheel, making strange noises that woke up Polly, who thought Bess had gone crazy yelling at Ken, and joined the melee. Anyway, they all survived and made it to North Carolina. Bess always ended her memory with: "Now you see why I call this "but for the grace of God" we all could have been at the foot of the mountain or rather in one of the ravines."

Ken is solely responsible for one of sister Ann's most terrifying moments as a child. According to her, when she had finally become brave enough to go fishing in a small boat on the little lake behind the house [actually it was just a pond provided by Papa for swimming and fishing], the boat suddenly starting rocking; she just knew she was about to be dumped into the water. Who was under the boat coming to her "rescue" but her devilish, grinning brother Ken, the perpetrator of the prank. [No doubt about it, he was born a schemer with a sense of humor, but never with malice.] Ann swears to this day that because of this early incident, she has never overcome her fear of water. She never learned to swim, either. Anybody who wanted to survive around Ken and water, learned to swim in that pond or in other swim holes. [Not much choice since ugly ole Jim Crow stole our chances of learning in public pools—if there were any in Hamlet.]

All the girls who shared the house with Ken felt the brunt of Ken's pranks and shrewdness. Kenny's sleeping quarters occupied a small room adjacent to the large bedroom where the girls slept. Frequently, after it was too dark for anybody to walk to the nearest store, a tempting smacking sound would emanate from Ken's room. Then followed the girls, converging on him, begging to share whatever he was so loudly enjoying. [The loud smacking was obviously designed for this purpose.] This was his time to make a few pennies off the drooling siblings. For a few extra pennies [beyond the cost of a one cent BB Bat sucker purchased by him earlier in the day] you could have the privilege of smacking with him. The longer you waited to make a deal, the more pennies you had to pay the "sucker" for his penny sucker. Polly's stubbornness and determination not to be outdone, earned her the highest prices. Sometimes, if you waited too long, you also had to return the used stick to Ken if it had "free" written on it. This meant that he could return it to the store for another piece of candy. It did not matter how many times this ritual took place, we always ended up being the real suckers! [Somehow, this boy just knew how to deal with people and come out on the winning end—most of the time.] As children of Papa Lee, we must have heard him frequently quote the Bible passage "Train up a child in the way he should go and he will not depart from it." I suspect we also heard Papa chuckle to himself as a clever "future business man" was seen leaving the house to hustle Grit newspapers when the bag he dragged along competed with his weight. [Ken was a little late starting on his growth.] This trait, determination to make it on his own, was only one of several characteristics the family observed in the early Kenny, as he was called in this inner circle. Another prominent trait shared by the family was/is a sense of humor and its ability to laugh no matter what. Papa and Mama saw to that. There was an old record that Papa played on the victrola when he felt it was needed. It was called simply, "The Laughing Record," and had nothing on it except peals and peals of laughter. Papa would offer a quarter [big money!] to anyone who could listen to it without laughing. Nobody ever got his quarter! [At times we could use that record now!]

2 Trick Photos of Ken and Wy as Children Made by Brother Alvis.
Wy Trapped in a Jar and The Giant Ken Holding Wy, the Tiny Captive, in His Hand

Kenny was always my favorite "man" after Papa. As the doting, unsuspecting, gullible baby sister [read stupid], I was the main recipient of his clever pranks—and they just kept coming [maybe still are]. Everything from not helping me with the dish washing by dropping one of Mama's old plates on the floor and hearing her say "Boy, get out of that kitchen." [which he did with a sly wink] to encouraging me to sing along with him [loudly, sometimes depending on what church we were in] modified hymns. "Nearer My God to Thee" became "Nero, my dog has fleas." Adults nearby just chuckled and pretended not to hear the PKs (preacher's kids) letting off a little steam. There were times on trips to country churches when acts of diplomacy were called for. The cooks who loved Papa and us [and wanted us to get fat] served hefty, delicious biscuits with huge centers and crusty outsides. We learned to bring the biscuits down to the edges of the table cloth, pull out the doughy centers, feed them to the cats under the table, return the crusty tops to our plates without the hosts [all entertaining the visiting minister] ever noticing what the diplomatic children and the well-fed, purring cats were enjoying. Each day of the early years of my life was filled with incidents initiated or provoked by brother Ken. [The preparation of this book is probably a continuation of his clever manipulation of me—filled with love, of course!] One special memory of our togetherness still weighs heavily on my heart; it was probably the first time I became aware of how much Ken really loved me.

We must have been 4 and 7 or 5 and 8 years old at the time. We both loved to fish in the backyard pond and in the creeks that wound through the woods beyond. [These were really supposed to be off-limits to me.] Ken seldom had the pleasure of going alone on his fishing trips; Baby "Wy" [nickname from when Winona was spelled Wynona] was always at his heels, to his disgust. I must have dropped behind a bit to avoid hearing his protests of "just go on back to the house" or "something bad is going to happen to you in these woods" etc., when a piercing scream shattered the silence. It came from me at the moment I felt a sharp pain in my knee. Love and fear kicked in and Ken dropped his pole, ran to me and started dragging me back to the house protesting all the way— "didn't I tell you," "Papa is going to kill me for letting something happen to his precious baby," "that was a poisonous spider that bit you" and on and on. [I forgot to mention that I was a Papa's girl as much as Ken was a Mama's shadow.] Anyway, Papa took care of the matter with his usual home-spun remedies, some of which were truly ingenious and Ken was not killed. Now I don't remember much about this incident, but having heard many versions of it, especially from Ken [who liked to add a little drama to things---- read exaggerate], the scar that remains on my knee never let me doubt that some terrifying thing happened that day. Since then, never have I doubted Ken's genuine love for me despite his harsh scolding and even though some older siblings swear that Ken tried to put me back in the doctor's bag shortly after I was born. [I was born at home in Hamlet in 1926.]

Even today, the three living sisters receive unexpected gifts of love from Ken such as a Mother's Day gift of a website for The Family Book. It seems that almost without being conscious of it he is still finding ways to honor the women in his life [read-- especially Mama and Nancy.] Two physical structures in Greensboro financed by Ken pay loving tribute to them—The Sarah Lownes Lee Senior Fitness Center as a part of the YMCA on East Market Street and The Nancy Young Lee Fellowship Hall at The New Directions Community Outreach Church.

These inner circle voices of the family say that J. Kenneth Lee, the man, did not just happen. Early characteristics and influences molded him into a brother to love, to remember, to be proud of, and to respect.

Lil's voice from a letter she wrote to Ken in 1984 [following an Honor for Nan] brings this section to an end. [It's a good thing we never throw anything away.]

Wed. Aug. 1, 1984

Hi,
This little note is late but from the heart. Thanks for the bulletin and program of your 25th Anniversary.

This seems to be Ken's year of long, over-due honors in that community. And I am happy to see Nan getting a little piece of the action also. It has been said "when a man climbs high on the ladder of success, standing at the foot of the ladder holding it steady, is his good wife". I believe that. I may not have quoted correctly but who cares. The wife deserves more honor than she receives usually — especially when it can't possibly take anything away from her husband, as in this instance. If I sound like a philosopher, it's because I am a self-made one (smiles). Congratulations again. I'm glad I know you (smiles).
Love you, Lil.

P.S. Program sounded beautiful.

Lee Home on Golf Course in Pinehurst, NC

The Lee House, Boathouse and Boat at Lake Tillary, NC

Lee Beach House at Topsail on Eastern Shores of North Carolina.
Later destroyed by 3 Hurricanes and Rebuilt

Group Boarding Private Plane for Hunting and Golf Trip at Invitation of Special Assistant to President Richard Nixon

No Way!

Voices of friends who were there—THEN

"I first met Ken in 1941 when he came to Greensboro to attend A. & T. College. I had enrolled in the Engineering program the year before and was here to welcome all the 'green' engineering students who came in 1941.

Ken and I had several things in common in addition to being engineering majors. We both selected Kappa Alpha Psi as our fraternity and since I had already been 'made', I got the pleasure of initiating Ken into Kappa Alpha Psi in his sophomore year. We also both lived in South Dorm and worked at the Pig and Whistle where, because of the 'condition of the times,' we had to do everything to survive—including a little 'stealing' now and then.

Very soon we became such good friends that we were sharing other important things such as courting, borrowing motorcycles and cars and everything else reckless, immoral, and illegal. It was about this time that Ken met Nancy at Bennett and I started going with Sabrina at A&T. Of course, they were two of an assortment of co-eds from N.C. Central, Winston-Salem State Teachers, Bluefield State, etc. As I remember there were only two cars on campus—a model A Ford owned by Little John and a Buick owned by Marable from Washington. By begging, borrowing and stealing we managed to get a car to make all the social functions at all the colleges along the Eastern Seaboard. Others in our gang were Alvin Blount, Russell Harris, John Gibson and others. Of course there was W. L. Kennedy trying to stabilize our restless natures and Max Thaxton 'giving us hell' in the math classes. But our main man was A.C. Bowling in Engineering—Bowling, a former boxing champion who used to threaten to use his pugilistic skills to keep us in line.

Those were hard times money-wise and we had to be shrewd to get finances; many of our plans for future financial adventures were born then—successes and failures. Then came the after-effects of Pearl Harbor and great changes in our college lives. I went the R.O.T.C route and Ken went to the Navy.

On one of his leaves home, Ken took the big step with Nan although we had memories of the blue Plymouth and the Artist Guild. Before too long, the next sight I saw was a little pregnant lady crossing the campus to visit Vivian Hayes and Roberta Favors and that was Nancy Lee and Mike Lee (to be.)

I stayed in the Army for a long period of 91 days and upon returning to college life, I got to know Nancy, Jim Young and Ion Young her father and mother. When Ken returned from the Navy he bought a small house on Lindsay near A&T and started his married life. Mike grew up filling a void that I had because I was away from my family and we can still remember many of his childhood incidents such as having to take him to Winston-Salem to get his gums cut for his teeth to come through.

At this time I had met my wife, Sabrina, and she and Nan became very close friends. Many cans of sardines and pork and beans were shared because of limited funds. We lived good with no money; had fun and tried anything. I got married and again had to assume some signs of maturity and responsibility.

Both Ken and I had returned to college and decided that this was time to start shaping our futures. At the insistence and prodding of A.C. Bowling we started using both our mental and physical facilities to provide for our families. Ken had completed his college requirements and gotten a position at his Alma Mater. On a $170 per month salary it was necessary for Ken and me to find other ways to supplement our income. I opened a radio repair shop and Ken opened a Record Shop with Nan as the sole employee on East Main Street that is now the site of the American Savings and Loan Association.

At that time, because there was inadequate training for Blacks in skilled areas, A.C. Bowling and Associates started Banneker Radio in Durham and Delwatt's Radio and Electronics Institute started in Winston-Salem by Ken and Associates with Wy as Secretary. Ken worked daily in Salisbury, Winston-Salem, and at A&T. I began working with Ken in Winston and that was the beginning of many of our joint ventures like the Forrest Lake Country Club, several radio shops in Greensboro and High Point, record and recording shops etc. In the late 50's we saw need for a Black Savings and Loan because of the absence of institutions willing to make loans to Blacks. In 1959 Ken and I, along with 8 others, organized the American Savings and Loan Association with an initial capital of $350,000; it has now grown to almost 11 million dollar operation.

Since both of us are very strong individualistic people we can always use each other's mind to hear our faults as well as our strengths. We disagree violently, but then we agree the same way. We are challenged by this. We both always love to see the rising sun when we travel together, which in recent years has become very frequent. This early morning rising has been very fruitful to us, though sometimes objectionable to our wives.

I guess I could best describe our friendship this way: I'd say when I look at the horizon of East Greensboro and remember Balky Bottom, Gilmer Street and all the slums east of the railroad tracks, it was Ken's imagination, guts and vision that started changes that can now be seen. I know him as a restless friend with a new idea and an innovative way of approaching every problem and we have never said to each other--'You can't do that,' Instead (we say) 'Always try to figure out the best way to get it done'.

Melvin T. Alexander
May, 1977

*****

Dear Friends,   March, 1976

I first met the Lee Family in 1932-33. I taught a class in Analytic Geometry at A&T College. Miss Lillian Lee (Ken's sister) was the only girl in the class. . . .

My next meeting with the Lee Family was in early 1940, when J. Kenneth Lee was a member of the electrical engineering class. He divided his attention between Greek Fraternities, editor of the student newspaper and electrical engineering studies. Early in life he showed the qualities that he needed to finish and practice law. ...

J. Kenneth organized the Forest Lake Country Club, American Federal Savings and Loan Association, Cumberland Shopping Center and many other real estate developments. He also has holdings in Atlanta and Nassau. In 1947, he organized, owned and headed Delwatt's Radio and Electronics School for veterans and continued it until 1954. He heads and manages a company located in Randolph, NC, and doing millions of business each year. He owns and manages one or more housing projects. In short, he's exceptionally adept at law, business, and finance.

When N.C. Mutual Life Insurance Company began building a new home office; they required all bidding companies to use minority labor in all branches of the construction. Four of my students in electrical engineering and I organized Consolidated Electric Company, bid on the job of wiring the building and wired it under the most adverse conditions. The quality of the work was most exceptional; the profit from the job was evenly divided with a joint company and the completed job a most satisfying one. As secretary of the company, the acumen of J. Kenneth Lee did much to make this possible.

In the early 1970's, J. Kenneth Lee was awarded a special plaque as A&T State University's most illustrious graduate for that year. J. Kenneth Lee, in turn, sent me the plaque and a letter praising my efforts and example with the electrical engineering students, saying that I deserved the plaque more than he did. He could not possibly have the gratitude for his award as I did for my gift.

In over forty years acquaintance with the Lee Family, I have found them to be unequal in education, ethics and business attainments. No facets of my life have been more enjoyed or more impressed with the accomplishments.

Sincerely,
A.C. Bowling

*****

March, 1976,
Hamlet, North Carolina

Dear Friends,

With a great deal of pride and satisfaction, I was privileged to have taught an exceptional man.

On a beautiful sunny morning in 1930, a six year old lad entered my classroom at Capital Highway School in Hamlet, NC. He came in seemingly full of energy, enthusiasm and curiosity. Added to those obvious traits was an air of confidence and aggressiveness which would have been a joy and challenge to any teacher. It was as if he had said, "here I am, and I'm ready for business." This bright and promising young man was John Kenneth Lee, who is the subject of a composition I wrote-entitled "Proudly I Taught." By the end of the first half of his first year, he had completed all of the work of the first grade. Such exceptional work was deserving of encouragement and reward. So, a trip to the Library, which was frequently made, and the second grade room furnished materials for the second half of the year. At the end of the school year, Kenneth was tested on the second grade work and came within a fraction of making a perfect score. The decision to promote him to the third grade was an easy one. It was not surprising then that when he finished the Capital Highway School eleven years later, he was Valedictorian of his class.

Sadie R. Jenkins

*****

March, 1976

Dear Friends,

As far as my memory permits me to reflect, I believe it was in the 1920's that I became acquainted with the H.F. Lee Family. My father and mother were members of the Church of God that Rev. Lee pastured. He organized the Church of God in Hamlet and was pastor there for many years. Not long after he started the work there, he moved his family to Hamlet and we have had a long, close relationship since then—a beautiful friendship that is a privilege which I hold most dearly.

Through the years, many of the Lee children were my students in high school mathematics. They were Lillian, Bessie, Ann, Polly, and Kenneth.

Kenneth was then, as he is now, a person with multiple interests. While in high school, he masterminded a project for me—painting the tin top of a small tenant house. He assembled the crew (two or three of his schoolmates), bought the paint, paid off the workers etc. I paid him but could not understand why it took so long to do the job. Later I found out that they had used TAR instead of paint. Anyway, after about forty years, that coating is still on the house. In 1974, when my life was torn asunder by the passing of my husband after 40 years together, who but Kenneth came to my assistance in clearing up my legal affairs. His patience and expertise meant everything to me. God bless him.

...

With love
Alice M. Thomas Nelson

*****

March, 1976

Dear Friends,

Reminiscing Kenneth Lee is a pleasure. Our friendship began in 1941 at North Carolina A&T University. We attended several of the same classes and enrolled in the Scroller Club of Kappa Alpha Psi Fraternity.

World War II interrupted our education. I joined the Army while Kenneth volunteered for service in the Navy. When I returned to A&T in 1946, he was a member of the teaching staff! He was excellent at teaching radio engineering,

We shared several business experiences. Our first, a woodyard was a financial disaster, but it was a lesson we never forgot. Our more successful ventures included an amplifier service, disc jockeying and a radio and electrical center.

Kenneth founded a veteran-approved school for training in radio and electronics in Winston-Salem, which flourished until he left to enter law school at UNC, Chapel Hill. He was one of the first Blacks to receive a law degree from this institution.

He returned to Greensboro to set up his law practice and showed a dedicated interest in community affairs, including an unsuccessful bid for the city council. Nevertheless his leadership ability proved itself through his unrelenting fight for pinpointing worthwhile business investments. He envisioned a shopping center and influenced several acquaintances to engage in forming a corporation, which led to a shopping complex on Market Street. Major businesses include an A&P Store, Building and Loan Association, a dry cleaning establishment, a professional building, and a service station.

Kenneth is an astute businessman and expanded his interest into area of housing and a nursing home. He is a generous person, well known for giving free legal consultations,

Being a family man is a source of inspiration for Kenneth. He enjoys home life with his lovely wife Nan, and son, Mike. This was exemplified even when he lived in a small home on Lindsay Street. The couple's genuineness was readily visible. Love, concern for others and sharing were evident despite their meager circumstances. There was, and still is, a closeness between the couple which has made it possible for them to weather sorrows and disappointments and to rejoice when triumphant. This has not changed as Kenneth achieved success.

Though small in stature, Kenneth is gigantic with vision, organizational and management skills, compassion and concern for other.

Sincerely,
John Gibson

*****

December 6, 1976

Dear Kenneth,

I don't know why, but recently and constantly I have been in a reminiscent mood, so much so that I have been unable to tackle my daily problems with the usual zeal and zest. It might just be old age.

As I sit here reflecting and turning back the mental pages, my thoughts go back particularly to the many pleasant memories of our long friendship over the last 25 years. I recall how I trusted you so wholeheartedly early in our friendship in taking a piggy-back ride on a motorcycle with a daredevil on a winding and curving road from Chapel Hill to Durham. Apparently our good friend Major High had this same kind of trust and confidence in you when he allowed himself to be a passenger on a small plane piloted by you that crashed in the back yard of a South Carolina Senator, en route to Atlanta. I guess both of us had the confidence that "you would really make it," as you have so successfully done in your many courageous and oftentimes unconventional ventures.

When Waldo Emerson said, "Who so would be a man must be a nonconformist," he must have perceived persons like yourself. The point is you always dared to be different. Really people who use their minds successfully ought not to be expected to pretend they are just like everybody else. If so they would lose the diversity from which springs all great ideas. Please believe me when I say that you have never robbed yourself of the precious quality of thinking for yourself no matter how unconventional it might be. This virtue causes you to stand very tall as a man and as my friend.

I am sure you can recall some of the following trying, challenging, and embarrassing incidents with which we were mutually faced from the beginning of our acquaintance as black law students:

1. Our State of North Carolina relegated and required us to attend the only Law School opened to us at North Carolina College in Durham. There we found three small classrooms in the Administration Building with another unshelved small room designated as the "Library" with old law books stacked on the floor.
2. The day we became the first black students to be admitted to the University of North Carolina Law School at Chapel Hill. We had trembling knees but eager minds seeking a good legal education.
3. Our first night as roommates in the "Buzzards Roost" of the dormitory at UNC. As you remember, we did not sleep at all for fear that the KKK would be marching up the stairs to get their bounty.

4. The first day we ate at the dining hall and found that we were not, in fact, the first Blacks to attend. We not only saw faces that were darker than ours, but we also saw faces from almost every foreign country in the world. Upon this, we both realized that our state had graciously given the opportunity for learning to complete strangers of this nation and state while requiring her two native sons to be admitted only by Court mandate. When we left the dining hall several law enforcement officers (with guns etc.) who were attending the Institute of Government, blocked the walkway for our normal passage to our dormitory. Before continuing our walk, we had a very short but deliberate conference. We decided within seconds that we would walk straight forward and die if need be in this effort. The Lord must have been with us, for as you remember, as we approached within two or three feet this human barrier, they departed like the waters of the Red Sea.
5. The conference we had with Chancellor House when he informed us that football games were for the general public and not necessarily for students. And that since we were colored we should allow ourselves to sit behind the goal posts where the other colored people sat. Of course, we told him in no unmistaken terms that we were students and would sit wherever we wished—and as you recall, we sat on the 50-yard line with card tricks at the UNC-Kentucky game.
6. At the graduation exercises (June, 1952), the late Governor Kerr Scott was the Commencement Speaker standing on a lighted platform in the middle of the football field, and the first thing he said was. "I have never in my life before seen so many educated people in the dark" (the stand seats were lighted).
7. When we took the bar examination as the first two black students from UNC and we tacitly agreed that "they" would not allow both of us (100%) to pass the examination at the same time. Yet we did make it on the first examination.

Kenneth, we have come a long way. Life has been truly good to us. However, I have some envy with love. Mike has blossomed into a fine young practicing lawyer under your capable hands—Harvey, Jr. is in the budding stage and all I can do is wait for the blossoms and the flowers.

Finally Kenneth, through all the hardships that we mutually encountered, I sincerely believed and devoutly prayed that the tumult and turbulence of those historic days represented agony and anguish through which we had to pass before we could behold the dawn of a new day of love, peace, freedom and justice. Many of our friends despaired when they had to behold the prejudices and persecutions of those tragic days, but I now view the present as a period preceding a new era when a new man and a new society will emerge. As we review the past of our people, we can see that they have shaken off the shackles of slavery and the restrictions of segregation. As history now unfolds itself, doesn't it seem reasonable to assume that we shall also overcome the sophisticated ordeal of prejudice and discrimination?

Sincerely,

Harvey E. Beech

*****

No Way!

March, 1977

Dear Friends,

I was a student in the University of North Carolina School of Law, Class of 1952. I was admitted in 1949 when the University was still a lily-white institution. Although I had previously lived in Greensboro for several years, I was not acquainted with Kenneth. Circumstances, however, were soon to make us both classmates and good friends.

A lawsuit, brought by several citizens of North Carolina that denied admission to the School of Law of their own state university, had been proceeding through the federal courts. As one who had been a dissenter on civil rights and other issues for some time, I was invited by the NAACP Council to meet with them in Durham in preparation for some of their appeals. I was in no way qualified to assist them on these grave legal issues but I could answer their questions about the extensiveness of the curriculum, the quality of the faculty in particular courses, the breadth of the library resources available at Chapel Hill, and other related matters in which they had great interest in preparation for oral argument. During the spring and summer of 1951 as an editor of the North Carolina Law Review and a class officer, I had encountered signs of growing tension amongst certain sectors of the law school faculty and student body. These were neither widespread nor generalized but very particularized. I recall one free-swinging discussion with Dean Henry P. Brandis who was a leader of the World Federalists. I encountered considerable upset and anger on his part when I pointed out the irony of his being interested in freedom and justice and democracy in the far parts of the world while he was the defendant in a suit brought for justice by fellow citizens of his own state. I inquired, I thought rather gently, at what point a man of principle would resign his position when faced with such conflict and contradiction in his seeming beliefs. As I recall the sharpness of that discussion was against the background of the final appeal of the case for admission of black students to the University of North Carolina.

When those students arrived at Chapel Hill in the fall of 1951, they were five in number and quite diverse in background and outlook. As I became acquainted with them individually, I was struck by the remarkable characteristics of Kenneth Lee. Already experienced in the business and professional world, he was adding legal training to the arsenal with which he could face the world. How he was able to maintain his famous smile bordering on a grin through the most aggravating of personal and collective circumstances remained a mystery to me. He was highly intelligent, superbly well-organized, decisive, dedicated and determined, impeccably honest and trustworthy, always the astute diplomat Against the most serious obstacles, faced with a quantum leap forward in academic demand and testing, and dealing with day-to-day problems of maintaining business contacts of a continuing character, and commuting to and from Chapel Hill, Kenneth managed to keep himself together, present a remarkably "cool" exterior to the world, successfully meet and manage the tough law school course requirements.

Above all, Kenneth has always been a warm, compassionate, caring man who was willing to give of himself to others. No one could have achieved what he did, without speaking of the vast civic and business interests in which he was later involved in Greensboro and elsewhere, without the constant support and backing which Nancy furnished. My wife and children have always valued, as I have, the warm friendship, the instant hospitality and the love of life and living characterized by Kenneth, Nancy and Michael.

Sincerely,
M. H. Ross

The Sound Of New Voices

The new millennium brought with it fresh young voices who would not let the world forget the legacy of J. Kenneth Lee. Four of these voices are captured here for posterity: one, as his secretary, had for several years observed Lee; one with a special tribute upon meeting him for the first time; one as a writer for the *Carolina Peacemaker*, the only African American Newspaper in the City; and one for the City's Daily Newspaper, the *Greensboro News and Record*. Each chose her own approach and style. All were inspired by Lee's determination in the face of adversity and his words, chosen by Nancy McLaughlin to end her feature story: "I don't believe you can make it if everybody else ain't making it. I know that's not the way you are supposed to say it, but it's the truth."

*****

Cynthia McAdoo was a young mother when she sought employment in the Law Office of Lee and Lee in 1977. Son Michael had graduated from North Carolina Central University and joined his father in the practice of law. Ironically, Michael had chosen to study at the college his father had left to integrate the UNC Law School in 1951. The Elder Lee had long since established his practice with his loyal secretary, Gladys H. Minor, who remained with him for over forty years until they both retired.

Several years later when changes began to take place in the Lee Family as a result of Michael's unexpected death and wife, Nancy's illness, Ken moved his office to his home and gradually began to reduce his general practice. Cynthia moved with Gladys and her "new boss" Kenneth whom she nicknamed "J.K." As work tapered off, "Bunny" (as she was called by all) was encouraged by her new boss to hone her employment credentials by returning to school to complete her bachelor's degree. Showing appreciation for Lee's foresight and support, she continued to work and enrolled at Greensboro College from which she graduated with honors in two and a half years. With further support and encouragement, she made the transition from Lee's firm to her present position.

As Executive Assistant at North Carolina A&T State University, she seized the opportunity to nominate J. K. Lee for the coveted honor of North Carolina A&T State University's Human Rights Medal. The Human Rights Medal is awarded annually by the University to recognize individuals who have endeavored to correct social injustice and have significantly contributed to the betterment of the world. The award was also established to honor individuals whose courageous actions are a reflection of the extraordinary action against social injustice that was demonstrated by the "NC A&T FOUR" and Sit-in Movement.

*****

In the midst of the 50-year celebration of the graduates of the UNC Law School (2002), a fresh young voice requested permission to be heard. The voice belonged to Tawanda Foster, a young woman just embarking on the road to a degree from the University of North Carolina Law School. Very few of those present knew who she was. We later learned that before receiving her Juris Doctor degree she would be the recipient of a Peter K. Daniel Memorial Scholarship, serve as staff writer for the First Amendment Law Review and serve on the Dean's Advisory Council. It did not take any of us long, however, to realize that here was a young woman well on her way to success--inspired, in her words, by the brave men who had opened the doors to a new world for her.

Her voice, filled with pride and compassion, silenced the room as she read a special poetic tribute to Beech and Lee (those present)--the black men who had made it possible for her to be standing among this group of distinguished lawyers. [Lee, re-reading the poem later, compared her original poem to the work of Maya Angelo.]

Tawanda received her Juris Doctor degree and was admitted to the North Carolina Bar in 2004. She immediately became actively involved in the committee work of Bar and Lawyers Associations. In four years she has moved from Law Clerk with the Equal Employment Opportunity Commission in Raleigh, to Assistant District Attorney for the Harnett County District Attorney's Office in Lillington, to her present position as Assistant Attorney General-Labor Section in Raleigh.

*****

The power and compassion of the words chosen by the writers for the two newspapers, Kitty J. Pope and Nancy McLaughlin, speak for themselves and tell us how much these young women are respected in the community. [Illustrations that enriched the latter story are omitted in this volume, unfortunately.]

The 44th Sit In Celebration Anniversary

"Promoting Social Change"

The Observance of the 44th Anniversary of the trail blazing "sit-down protest" at the
F. W. Woolworth lunch counter on Monday, February 1, 1960,
by the A&T Four: Franklin McCain, David L. Richmond, Joseph McNeil
and Ezell Blair Jr., later known as Jibreel Khazan

January 30, 2004

Sponsored by the Division of Student Affairs
Dr. Roselle L. Wilson, Vice-Chancellor

North Carolina Agricultural and Technical State University
Greensboro, North Carolina 27411

Human Rights Medalist Recipient

J. Kenneth Lee

J. Kenneth Lee, a longtime civil rights attorney, had contributed immensely to the enrichment of the lives of African Americans and the underprivileged throughout this state and nation. Atty. Lee graduated valedictorian from Hamlet Colored School in Hamlet, N.C. In 1941, he entered North Carolina A&T College with the $33 that his father, a minister, had saved to pay for his first semester. Lee graduated from A&T in 1945 with a B.S. degree in electrical engineering and later was awarded an honorary Doctorate of Laws degree from his alma mater.

In 1951, he made history by being one of three African Americans to be admitted to the University of North Carolina at Chapel Hill law school. He and his classmates were admitted under a Supreme Court ruling allowing blacks to be admitted to white professional schools. The students were accompanied to class by law enforcement officers, lived in segregated housing, were given used books and were never referred to in class by their names. Lee endured all of these injustices and in 1952, received his J.D. from the university. He has since been honored by UNC-CH for his outstanding scholastic record and contributions to the legal profession.

Lee is to be noted for his outstanding contributions to the legal profession. As assistant legal counsel for the State NAACP, a position for which he received no pay, Lee filed suit after suit to integrate facilities of the state. One of his most notable suits was filed in 1957. He represented five black children who were suing the Greensboro City Schools for admission to the all white Gillespie Park Elementary School. He won the suit and his action opened the doors of the Greensboro City Schools to African Americans.

This great humanitarian has represented in excess of 1,700 original Sit-In demonstrators as defendants in both original trials and appeals without any compensation or fees. Lee has a lot of firsts in front of his name. His firsts include being appointed by the governor to the NC State Banking Commission and to the NC State Housing Finance Agency; and being inducted into the Greensboro Business Leaders Hall of Fame.

Lee is the founder, president and chairman of the Board of Directors for 30 years at The American Federal Savings and Loan Association of Greensboro; founder and president of a 100 bed skilled nursing facility, Medical Care Inc.; founder of the A&T Alumni Association. Lee is the Builder of the Cumberland Shopping Center, which is now the location for the Dudley-Lee Business Building. He is a charter member of the first integrated Greensboro Housing Foundation.

In 1998, Lee received UNC-CH Distinguished Alumni Award and in 2002 the NC State Bar Certificate of Appreciation for 50 years or more of service. He is married to Nancy Young. They had a son, Michael who is now deceased. The Lees have three grandchildren.

Cynthia D. McAdoo
3006-B Darden Road
Greensboro, NC 27407

7 November 2003

Committee for Awards, Honorary Degrees,
 and Founders/ Honors Day
c/o Office of the Chancellor
1601 East Market Street
Greensboro, NC 27411

**RE: Nomination of J. Kenneth Lee for
 Human Rights Medal**

Dear Awards Committee:

It is with great pleasure and honor that I nominate J. Kenneth Lee for the North Carolina Agricultural and Technical State University's 4th Annual Human Rights Medal.

Mr. Lee was born the 13th child in a family whose father was a Black Minister. He grew up during the Depression years, a time which he believed set the stage for most of the obstacles and adversities he has fought throughout his life. With a determination "not to be run out of the South", Mr. Lee took risks and was willing to be on the cutting edge of controversy to help Blacks overcome southern prejudices.

His accomplishments and awards are numerous as he used his position as a lawyer to gain access to important information and plans affecting Black people in his community as well as the State.

Proudly, I list some of his accomplishments and awards:

> He enrolled at NC A&T in 1941 with $33.00 his father saved to pay for his First semester and earned a degree in Electrical Engineering and awarded an Honorary Doctorate degree from his alma mater.

> In 1953, Mr. Lee was one of four black students admitted to UNC-Chapel Hill, an all White law school. He later recalled that they were accompanied to class by law enforcement officers, segregated and housed on the 4th floor of an all white dormitory, given used books for studying and never called by their names while attending class.

He devoted his law practice to civil rights cases during the late 1950s and 1960s. He was Assistant Legal Counsel for the state NAACP, a position that made him local counsel in the first lawsuits to integrate elementary and secondary public schools. In 1957, he successfully represented five black children in a lawsuit against the Greensboro City Schools seeking admission to an all white school. His clients were the first black students in North Carolina to attend an all-white school.

He represented the majority of the 1,700 civil disobedience cases in North Carolina during the Civil Rights Marches in Greensboro. One case was of particular concern to him; the case of his own son, Mike.

He is the former President and Chairman Emeritus of American Federal Savings and Loan Association which was the first black federally chartered savings and loan association. Mr. Lee says that built on faith (and small deposits) of 530 shareholders from the community, the bank created a new major economic developmental resource for the community. A large number of black owned homes in the city now attests to the impact this venture has had on the entire community.

Mr. Lee's continuing obsession for improving the quality of living for neglected minorities compelled him to create an environment where Black professionals could practice their learned trades. Subsequently, he built Cumberland Shopping Center, which housed office space for 5 physicians, 6 lawyers, an architect, a drug store, 2 insurance companies, 2 real estate agencies and a trading stamp company.

Years later, with financial support from Housing and Urban Development (HUD), he developed the Lincoln Grove Shopping Center, which HUD cited as an outstanding project under its Urban Development Action Grant. In addition to Lincoln Grove Shopping Center, he helped to renovate L. Richardson Memorial Hospital, the state's only black hospital, into a 100 bed skilled nursing care facility, the majority of whose patients were indigent and welfare recipients.

I have had the pleasure of working with Mr. Kenneth Lee in his law firm for some twenty plus years and have witnessed some of his triumphs in his efforts to improve the lives of others.

I have attached supporting newspaper articles and photographs as supporting documentation. Any favorable consideration given this nomination would be greatly appreciated.

Very truly yours,

Cynthia D. McAdoo

Enclosures

BUNNY McADOO
3006-B Darden Road
Greensboro, NC 27407

20 October 2003   **HAND DELIVERED**

Rev. Howard Chubbs
Mr. Marvin Watkins
Greensboro, NC

RE: Nomination of J. Kenneth Lee for
NC A&T Annual Human Rights Medal

Dear "HEROS"

Hi! As you can see from the reference above, I am attempting to nominate JK for this award and need your help!

As you can see from the application, the Awards Committee will be looking for an individual who has had a positive impact on correcting social injustices and other humanitarian services. Who deserves to receive this award more than JK? (okay, so I am a little prejudice :-)

Your task, if you accept, is to write a letter of reference to support my nomination. You must be as familiar with JK's accomplishments as I am, but if not, attached are some of the high moments in his legendary career.

I can be reached at (336) 547-8220 (h) or (336) 334-7592 (w).

Thank both of you in advance for your cooperation and I look forward to hearing from you.

Very truly yours,

Bunny

/attachments

Lee With Coveted Human Rights Medal from NCA&T Awarded in 2005

NORTH CAROLINA AGRICULTURAL AND TECHNICAL STATE UNIVERSITY

N. RADHAKRISHNAN (RADHA) PhD, P.E.
INTERIM VICE CHANCELLOR FOR RESEARCH

November 7, 2003

Committee For Awards, Honorary Degrees, and
   Founders/Honors Day
North Carolina A&T State University
1601 East Market Street
Greensboro, NC 27411

Dear Committee Members:

    This letter is written in support of the nomination of Mr. J. Kenneth Lee, long-time lawyer, businessman, civil rights leader, community activist and resident of Greensboro, N.C., to be the next recipient of the Annual Human Rights Medal awarded by North Carolina Agricultural and Technical State University.

    Attorney J. Kenneth Lee, in my opinion, embodies the totality of the eligibility criteria for being honored with this most prestigious award. I cite for example, as a young adult, he, along with two other young men had the foresight and courage to make application to the then all white School of Law at The University of North Carolina at Chapel Hill. He was approved for admission and in 1952 became one of the first two Black Americans to graduate from a white law school in North Carolina. Within one year following graduation he was appointed to the key position as Assistant Legal Counsel for the state office of the National Association For The Advancement of Colored People (NAACP). Attorney Lee was involved, in one way or the other, with almost every civil rights or discrimination case brought in the state from 1953 until all of them were victorious. At one point in time Attorney Lee had more than 1,700 active civil rights cases awaiting trial.

    Not only did Attorney Lee possess a keen legal mind but also one that personifies being an active participant in the American free enterprise system. In the 1950's period it was almost impossible for Black Americans to obtain home mortgage loans from banks in North Carolina above the $13,500 threshhold. The practice of redlining Black Americans loan applications was very much in vogue. Attorney Lee had an answer for that situation also. The answer he said was to establish our own bank. Mr. Lee, along with several other Black community leaders, in 1959, founded the American Federal Saving and Loan Association Bank in Greensboro. This resulted in an unprecedented number of Black Americans becoming homeowners.

A Land-Grant University and A Constituent Institution of the University of North Carolina
Division of Research • 1601 East Market St. • Greensboro, NC 27411 • (336) 334-7314 • Fax (336) 334-7086

Letter of Support
Page 2
November 7, 2003

    Attorney Lee's caring attitude and disposition can best be exemplified by action he took in 1967 to save the last black administered hospital in the State of North Carolina. In order to keep the facility from being razed, he solicited support from friends, purchased the hospital and then converted it into a 100-bed skilled nursing care facility.

    Additionally, Attorney Lee has contributed both his time and his financial resources to assisting North Carolina A&T State University, Bennett College for Women and the local Hayes Taylor Branch of the YMCA. His obsession for improving the lives of Black Americans and other minorities has led him to strive for better housing, equal job opportunities, better health care for the young and old, improved learning conditions at all levels of education and just a burning desire or willingness to be of assistance to the less fortunate citizens of our community, state, and country.

    Again, in view of the foregoing realities, I respectfully and enthusiastically support the nomination of Attorney J. Kenneth Lee for the next Annual Human Rights Medal Award.

                                             Sincerely,

                                             Marvin H. Watkins
                                             Special Assistant to the Interim
                                             Vice Chancellor For Research

PROVIDENCE BAPTIST CHURCH
1106 Tuscaloosa Street
Greensboro, North Carolina 27406
Telephone: (336) 273-7552
Telecopier: (336) 273-0150

Howard Allen Chubbs, D. Min., D.D.
Senior Minister

November 10, 2003

Committee for Awards, Honorary Degrees, and Founders/Honors Day
c/o Office of the Chancellor
North Carolina A & T State University
1601 East Market Street
Greensboro, NC 27411

To The Committee for Awards:

I am honored to nominate J. Kenneth Lee as a candidate for the fourth Annual Human Rights Medal to be awarded by the University at the 44th Anniversary of the Greensboro Sit-In Movement.

In consideration of the criteria for nomination and the previous recipients of the award, Mr. Lee has contributed immeasurably to the betterment of the lives of African Americans, not only in the Greensboro community but his efforts have impacted their lives throughout the nation. A graduate of North Carolina A & T State College (at the time of his matriculation), Mr. Lee was one of the first two African Americans to be admitted to and finish the University of North Carolina Law School. He has since been honored by the University for his outstanding scholastic record and contributions to the legal profession.

But it was his contributions to the improvement of the lives of African Americans and other underprivileged citizens that make Mr. Lee an obvious candidate. As assistant legal counsel for the State NAACP, a position for which he received no pay, Mr. Lee filed suit after suit to integrate facilities of the state. The most notable of such suits was in 1957 when he successfully represented five black children suing the Greensboro City Schools for admission to all white Gillespie Park Elementary School. This action opened the doors of the Greensboro City Schools to African Americans. During the Sit-In Demonstrations represented the majority of the 1,700 civil disobedience cases in North Carolina, again without pay. In 1959, because white banks would not make mortgage loans to blacks, he helped to organized American Federal Savings and Loan Association which made home ownership possible for many Blacks for the first time. Mr. Lee also developed and assisted in the development of affordable housing and business opportunities for Black entrepreneurs and under funded minorities. Not to be excluded, Mr. Lee has been a consistently great contributor of free legal advice and monetary support to his alma mater, A& T State University.

I am confident that all of the nominees for the Award are deserving, but I am also convinced that none are more worthy or represent the intent and qualifications of the award than Mr. J. Kenneth Lee. I hope that you agree.

Sincerely,

Howard Allen Chubbs

HAC:brh

The Arrival

For Mr. Harvey Breech and Mr. Kenneth Lee and Mr. Floyd
    McKissick in Celebration of the 50th Anniversary of Their
    Integration and Graduation from UNC LAW

    fifty years ago
you came
    to an UN-WELCOMING brave new world
you came
    breaking and shattering stereotypes
you came
    to open doors for US

    fifty years ago
you came
    waging war against injustice
you came
    fighting with minds determined and hearts of hope
you came
    walking through hell's fire with feet planted and protected only by
God

    fifty years ago
you came
    amid a whirlwind of insults and indignities
you came
    refusing to be separated and ignored
you came
    refusing to return the pool privilege card accidentally issued to you
you came

    fifty years ago
you came
    preserving and enduring a pain cutting so deep no amount of accolades
    and ceremonies can erase the pain of those memories
you came
    offering your heart and soul and sometimes even your body to be the first

No Way!

    to run the gauntlet being pummeled by their ignorance and the resistance
    to integration

you came
    bearing that pain so that I wouldn't have to

    fifty years ago
you came
    to a place that tried to force you to stand on the outside
but you came
    inside this place
    strong and wise
    forceful and righteous
    standing tall and refusing to bow down
    opening doors and blazing trails
    changing the tides of Dixie

    fifty years ago
you came
    so that one day I could come
you came and you stood

    and no man can deny that you came
    and no history book can deny that you came
    and we your legacy will not allow them to forget that you came

and we your legacy are thankful for your coming
and we your legacy honor you for coming
and we your legacy pay tribute to you for coming

    fifty years ago
you came
    opening the door wide enough
    for US to come.

Copyright October 30, 2002, Tawanda N. Foster

GREENSBORO NEWS & RECORD

Copyright (c) 2002, Greensboro News & Record, Inc.

Sunday, March 24, 2002
BY NANCY MCLAUGHLIN~ Staff Writer
SECTION: THE POWER OF ONE
MAN UNDETERRED BY SYSTEM STACKED AGAINST HIM
GREENSBORO

The police called it "reckless eyeballing."

A black man working in an Alamance County tobacco field had stopped what he was doing to watch as a white woman walked by.

"He didn't say anything to her; she didn't say anything to him," says Kenneth Lee. "The police called it assault."

The year was 1953. As the man's attorney, Lee argued there was no such thing as "reckless eyeballing." The judge, who came to court in bibbed overalls and with no legal training, gave the man two years anyway.

"People won't believe it," Lee says. "Today we don't think these kind of things could have ever happened."

He had that same reaction once.

"When I was little I used to get on my grandma's knee and she used to tell me about how they treated her as a slave, and I didn't believe her because I didn't think people would be that mean," Lee says.

Lee, who lives in Greensboro, would learn firsthand the depths of human unkindness and the means to overcome it in a life that spanned a time of tremendous social change in this country. A black man born into a segregated world, he would nonetheless become a lawyer, a businessman and a civil rights legend. He didn't do it by smashing through the walls that blocked his way, or hoisting himself over the top. Quietly and resolutely, he chiseled out a doorway that everyone could use.

Fifty years ago, he and Harvey Beech of Kinston became the first black men to graduate from the law school at UNC-Chapel Hill. It would be the first of many firsts that Lee would achieve in a life that charts the progress of civil rights in America. The letter confirming his admission is among a collection of papers he's donating to the planned International Civil Rights Museum, because he doesn't want people to forget there was a time when black people didn't count in the eyes of the law.

Henry Frye, the first black state supreme court chief justice; Julius Chambers, retired chancellor of N.C. Central University in Durham; and Bob Brown, a black former assistant to President Richard Nixon, are among those who walked through doors Lee opened.

"He's brilliant, tenacious, a multi-talented giving and serving lawyer and businessman who never forgot where he came from, who was always reaching out and reaching back to help others," says Brown. A policeman in the 1960s, Brown often had a front-row view of Lee in the courthouse. Today, Brown is president of an international public relations firm.

"He made a lot of steps and raised the hope of a lot of black people who saw him do it," Brown says. "And we felt we could do it, too."

A stroke incapacitated Lee in August, keeping him in the hospital for three months, unaware as

No Way!

pictures of the World Trade Center towers and the Pentagon ablaze became forever ingrained in the American psyche. As anthrax became a household word. As the stock market bottomed out.

"Imagine going to sleep with $20 and waking up with 10 cents," Lee says jokingly, as he moves around the bottom floor of his home using a newfangled three-wheeled walker.

The stroke has done little to strip Lee of his humor, his recollection of events, or those eyes that dance as he talks of righted wrongs. His youthful face belies 78 years and countless struggles.

His roots stretch back to Charlotte, where he was born in 1923, the 13th of 14 children. His father, a Church of God minister making $11 a week, moved the family to Hamlet when he was 3. The elder Lee made sure his sons learned to use their minds as well as their hands, and that his daughters would be educated and wouldn't work in anybody's kitchen but their own.

At dinner, Lee's mother would sometimes busy herself and insist the family start without her. Lee once crept to the wood stove where she kept her plate and saw the small portions.

"I knew I had to try to do something to give my mother every material thing she ever wanted," Lee says. It became one of the greatest motivators in his life.

Lee graduated valedictorian of a class that met in a church and never had access to a library. He enrolled at N.C. A&T in 1941, with $33 his father had scraped and saved to pay for his first semester.

When he moved into the dorm, it was the first time he had lived in a place with electricity and running water.

"I remember the first time the chemistry professor asked me to go to the lab and get a Bunsen burner," Lee says. "I had never been in a lab all my life."

Lee was set to earn a degree in electrical engineering after just three years of study, but World War II intervened. He joined the Navy, and during training married girlfriend Nancy Young, then a senior at Bennett College. He served in the Pacific on the USS Dade, an attack transport ship with segregated eating and sleeping quarters.

Nancy wrote him every day about the child they were expecting.

Honorably discharged after two years, Lee returned to A&T and finished his last few months, earning a degree in electrical engineering in 1946.

But he couldn't get hired - even though jobs for qualified engineers filled the want ads.

"They said their policy was to follow the tradition of the neighborhoods," Lee says. And in the South in the 1940s, that meant segregation.

It was devastating.

"Each time he reached what he thought was good enough, the doors would close in front of him," says his youngest sister, Winona Fletcher.

He went to work at A&T as a professor in electrical engineering, but the "tradition of the neighborhoods" gnawed away at him.

"Black people were doing all kinds of crazy things to exist," he says. They sat at the back of the bus and went to the back door of restaurants to be served. Black people with degrees had to accept lesser jobs.

"It was hell certified by law. We knew that if you stayed on your side of the fence you could avoid the nastiness of segregation," Lee says. "But who wanted to live that way?"

Lee thought the only way out of segregation was through the legal system, so he began to think about law school.

A few years earlier, the National Association for the Advancement of Colored People had begun legal action to integrate UNC's law school. But the case took so long to wind its way through the legal system that by the time it got to court, the original plaintiffs were about to graduate law school at the North Carolina School for Negroes (now North Carolina Central University), making their cases moot.

Lee applied to the Durham school and signed on as a plaintiff in the case against UNC.

In Durham in 1949, he found secondhand law books stacked from floor to ceiling in no particular order in the one-room school.

"When you wanted a book, you had to find it, take all the books on top of it off, and then stack the rest of them back when you were done," Lee says. "I didn't want a legal education that way."

The case went to court in 1950, with Thurgood Marshall representing the plaintiffs. Marshall, who would go on to become the first black U.S. Supreme Court justice, was then chief legal counselor with the NAACP's Legal Defense Fund.

Though Marshall dismantled the arguments for separate but equal, the judge ruled against them, saying, " 'I know ya'll should be admitted to the UNC law school, but someone other than me will have to sign it,' " Lee recalls.

"It was the times," says Lee. "You had Jesse Helms on WRAL talking about niggers forcing their way into Chapel Hill."

The U.S. Court of Appeals sided with the plaintiffs and the U.S. Supreme Court refused to hear the case.

A contingent of police officers escorted Lee and Beech to the campus dining hall that first day in 1951.

"Everybody stopped, forks in mid-air," Lee says.

Within a few days, the black students drew little attention. Often, white students would sneak onto their floor so they could study together. As the only black students, Lee and Beech had a floor to themselves.

"The worst thing about segregation and discrimination is what it did to a man's mind from birth," Beech says.

The devil, Lee says, was always in the details.

In a class where students sat alphabetically and had to recite case law, the professor addressed each of them in order and by name, using the title, "mister."

"He would get to me and just point," Lee says. "He just couldn't bring himself to call me mister.

"It hurt every time," Lee admits. "Some things would make me angry, but I found out when you get angry, you can't do a damn thing else. I found that a lot of people that I should have hated I never did. What good would it have done me?"

Lee's graduation from law school in 1952 was far more understated than his entrance: His degree came in the mail. Lee passed the bar exam before graduation and skipped the ceremony. He had work to do back home.

That 1953 conviction for reckless eyeballing would be reversed on appeal - a path Lee would have to take many times as he found out how tough it was to be a black lawyer.

Lee often found himself arguing before jurors who would rather look out the window than at him. Lee argued his first jury case while a spectator sat in the courtroom with a double-barreled shotgun sticking out from under his trouser leg.

"The judge saw it, the other attorneys saw it, I saw it - and nobody said anything about it the whole time," he says.

The case involved five black men charged with killing a white sheriff's deputy in Moore County. The attorney general's office had sent two attorneys to prosecute, and a couple of lawyers running for statewide offices also volunteered their time.

The young men had committed the crime, and Lee hoped only to spare them the death penalty.

He had the law on his side; the men hadn't been arraigned properly. As the three-week trial neared its end, he handed the judge a brief.

"The judge called us all into his chambers. He said, now here I've got a bench of lawyers with 200 years of experience and here is a boy on his way out of law school. You let me sit here three weeks and make a fool out of myself. You go back and work out a plea or I'll let them all go."

The man who pulled the trigger got life in prison.

Much of his time in the late 1950s and early 1960s was devoted to civil rights cases. Lee was serving as assistant legal counsel for the state NAACP, a position that none of the state's other 30 to 40 black lawyers really wanted.

"It was dangerous for anybody who advocated the rights of minorities," Frye says. "It was dangerous to be questioning any white person."

His position with the NAACP made Lee local counsel in the first suits brought in the state to integrate elementary and secondary public schools.

In 1957, Lee successfully represented five black children suing the Greensboro City Schools for admission to all-white Gillespie Park elementary. They, along with Josephine Boyd, who entered Greensboro Senior High at the same time, became among the first black students in the state to attend previously all-white schools.

"It was hard to get a parent to put his child in that kind of situation," says Lee, who argued cases in a steady, compelling voice. "People were getting lynched for just trying to eat in a restaurant. What they did was special and took a lot of guts. It wasn't anything I did."

Lee also represented the majority of the 1,700 civil disobedience cases in North Carolina that started with the Woolworth sit-ins of 1960 and included the arrest of his own son, Michael.

"I never got paid for a single one of them," Lee says, smiling. "I called the NAACP for a little help and Thurgood Marshall said to me, 'We spent half a million dollars getting you into law school. It's time for payback.' "

The integration suits, which would expand to swimming pools, golf courses and other public venues, eventually brought an end to Jim Crow laws.

Lee keeps a copy of a postcard someone sent anonymously during those years, inviting Lee and all his friends to move north. Postcards were the least of it.

"We went through the cross burnings and the fires and the nights that we didn't think he'd come home," Michael Lee once said. "I remember when I was very small we used to get phone calls saying he had been shot ... or had been tied to a stake and would not be coming home."

Through it all, Kenneth Lee was resilient.

"My wife was strong and Michael grew to understand that there were people who were desperate to have things stay the way they were," Lee says.

Perhaps nothing reflects more clearly the contradictions in race relations of the era as Lee's relationship with a Ku Klux Klan leader named Clyde Webster. A carpenter by trade, Webster marched with KKK banners on the day black children integrated Gillespie Park School, and later threw bottles through the plate glass window of Lee's office.

Webster was given an active jail sentence for the vandalism. His case was on appeal when he showed up at Lee's office one day.

"He said, 'I was fired,' "Lee recalls. Webster happened to be the chief carpenter for the company Lee had just hired to build his home. Knowing the history between the two, the company fired Webster. "He said, you and me ain't gonna never agree on race, but I'm the best damn carpenter you will find and I will save you money. You won't have to speak to me if you don't want to."

Though he's still not sure why, Lee agreed to let Webster stay on the job. During the construction, the men often talked - but Lee never changed Webster's views about race.

Lee's home had been completed by the time Webster's appeal came up and Webster's lawyer subpoenaed Lee to talk about the time the two men had spent together. As a result, Webster was given a suspended sentence.

They saw each other just outside the courtroom. Webster, surrounded by other KKK members, reached out his hand to Lee.

"He said, 'I just want to let you know that if anybody in this town ever messes with you, all you've got to do is call us.' "

Lee saw it as an "unholy alliance," but the harassment and phone calls stopped.

When school opened the next fall, Webster was back picketing in front of Gillespie with a 4-foot-high sign saying, "NIGGER GO HOME."

"He looked over toward the street, saw me passing, threw up his hand and hollered as loud as he could, 'Hey Mr. Lee, how you been doing?' "

Lee never made a lot of money as a lawyer.

It was business acumen and initiative that ensured him a comfortable life, including homes on the golf course in Pinehurst and the oceanfront in the Caribbean.

"Kenneth always had a good sense for business," Winona Fletcher says, laughing. In the first grade, her brother won a bike delivering a weekly farmer's almanac. He used it to ride several miles to a country store, where he bought penny lollipops that he would resell to his siblings for a few cents more.

As an adult, he turned racism into opportunity. Where segregation shut out black people, he found a way to open another door, often making a profit and creating jobs in the process. In the 1940s, for example, black people couldn't go to white theaters to see black performers such as Duke Ellington. So Lee also opened a theater in Salisbury.

In the years after World War II, A&T had more engineering applicants than space. So in 1947, Lee set up his own radio and electronics trade school in Winston-Salem, and filled it with black veterans seeking education through the GI Bill.

He maintained those businesses and others during law school with the help of his wife, Nancy, who had earned degrees from Bennett and A&T, and was a teacher at Price Elementary.

Lee's business ventures were doing well by the time he went to the bank to borrow $20,000 - the remainder he needed to build a $55,000 house in what would become Benbow Park.

"They told me they didn't loan black people more than $13,000," Lee says. "Nobody was bashful then."

Not believing the loan officer, Lee researched mortgage loans at the courthouse and found just one bank loan to a black man for $13,500.

At a time when established financial institutions in the city had no black people as managers or even tellers, Lee contacted the Federal Home Loan Bank Board and told them he wanted to charter a savings and loan.

"It took a lot of initiative, a lot of nerve, a lot of planning, and Kenneth was good at that," Frye says.

American Federal opened in 1959 as the first black federally-chartered savings and loan in the state.

The savings and loan enabled more black people to build homes, and soon white financial institutions released restrictions on black customers in order to compete.

"It was the first time blacks could build a brick house - that was monumental," says Lewis

Brandon, a retired science teacher and former sit-in participant. "When you would go there, you would see people from all walks of life, people with mud on their shoes and in coveralls from working all day. It was their bank."

Once black people had homes, they had collateral to get loans to start businesses. Lee served as the unpaid president of the savings and loan for 30 years.

"He saw the need for things to be done," Brandon says, "and he just did them."

In the late 1960s, Lee got President Richard Nixon to call the chairman of the A&P grocery chain, who then agreed to anchor the Cumberland shopping center Lee was developing near A&T. It was believed to be the first time the chain located one of its stores in a black shopping center anywhere across the South. Brown, the former police officer, was by then one of the president's assistants.

Lee helped develop the Lincoln Grove Shopping Center on McConnell Road, and founded Carolina Nursing Center, the state's first and largest black-owned nursing facility.

Lee was the first black person to serve on the state's banking commission in 1973, and the first black business person inducted in the Greensboro Business Leaders Hall of Fame in 1985.

Lee, a Republican, ran for public office just once. He won in the primary for City Council in the early 1950s, the same year William Hampton, a black Greensboro doctor, also ran. Lee was hearing that two black men wouldn't make it on the City Council, so he pulled out before the general election. He never ran again because he realized he didn't like all the attention.

"I walk out on the street," Lee says, "and nobody knows who I am."

His office says it all.

There's the "Colored" sign he removed from the segregated bathrooms in the Guilford County courthouse in the 1950s. A plaque names him a founding member of the Southeastern Lawyer's Association, a professional group for black lawyers. There are many others that reflect his influence in law, civil rights, business and community.

Lee is most proud of the one that marks his efforts in issuing $2.2 billion tax-exempt bonds that built more than 55,000 new houses for low- to moderate-income families in service with the North Carolina Housing Finance Agency.

"After the students were able to eat where they wanted to and could go to a movie when they wanted to, my thoughts turned toward their parents," Lee says. "We still had people living in Greensboro like we did in Hamlet years ago, with no indoor plumbing or electricity."

These days, Lee spends his time surfing the Internet, reading several daily newspapers, and keeping involved in the community.

But his pace is slowing.

In May, he is closing his investment office, the last vestige of his multifaceted career. Lee doesn't drive much - mostly to the doctor's office or to visit his wife, Nancy, who has Alzheimer's disease and had to be placed in a highly-skilled nursing home after his stroke.

"That's the worse thing that could have happened to me," he says softly, sadness creeping into his voice.

It is the first time in 60 years of marriage that they have spent more than a couple of nights apart.

Lee has lived long enough to lose both his parents and his son. His mother died during his freshman year at A&T, never knowing what he would accomplish. He helped build the Sarah Lee Fitness Center at the Hayes-Taylor YMCA in her honor. Michael, who followed his father into the legal profession, died of a heart attack in 1995. The legal legacy continues through his granddaughter, Michele Bonds.

He also has lived long enough to see some of the things he built - such as the Cumberland Shopping Center - fall into disrepair after it passed from his hands.

But always, life moves on. A new office complex is going up on the land where the Cumberland once sat, part of the biggest building spree along East Market Street in decades.

It will be called the Dudley-Lee Complex in honor of Lee and his son, and Dudley Products founders Joe and Eunice Dudley.

The doorways he helped chisel through the wall of prejudice have been enlarged by those who followed him, people such as Henry Frye and Julius Chambers. And if the doorway keeps getting larger, maybe one day there won't be a wall anymore.

"I don't believe you can make it if everybody else ain't making it," Lee says. "I know that's not the way you are supposed to say it, but it's the truth."

Contact Nancy H. McLaughlin at 373-7049 or nmclaughlin@news-record.com
PHOTOS BY JAMES PARKER/ News & Record
Retired lawyer and businessman Kenneth Lee, who fought many civil rights cases in his career, recently donated his papers to the planned International Civil Rights Museum. Lee removed this "colored" sign - which now hangs on his office bathroom door - from the segregated bathrooms in the Guilford County courthouse in the 1950s. He calls segregation "hell certified by law."

In 1951, Kenneth Lee and Harvey Beech of Kinston became the first black students admitted to the UNC-Chapel Hill law school. This copy of Lee's acceptance letter is part of his donation to the proposed civil rights museum.

Retired lawyer Kenneth Lee was one of the black students first admitted to the UNC-Chapel Hill law school. Lee says he knew the legal system was the only way out of segregation and fought many civil rights cases.

CAROLINA PEACEMAKER, THURS., FEBRUARY 8 thru WED., FEBRUARY 14, 1996

John Kenneth Lee:
ADVERSITY'S LESSONS

By Kitty J. Pope
Freelance Writer

The story of John Kenneth Lee is one of struggle as well as triumph. A man of dedication, integrity and compassion, J. Kenneth Lee has managed to overcome obstacles and hardships to achieve his goals and visions.

Now in retirement, his career spanned from electrical engineer to civil rights attorney to founder and president of First American Federal. "I've always been a person of determination," says Lee, "which must have played a major part in whatever successes I have achieved in life."

The grandson of a slave, Lee says that he encountered thousands of obstacles in life because he is black, some of which he was able to surmount. One of fourteen children, he remembers both parents being inspirational to his success. "Father always sent me religious quotations and my mother took pride in my accomplishments. Both had faith in me and encouraged me to reach my goals," explains Lee.

Fascinated by his father's and brothers' mechanical abilities, Lee decided to study electrical engineering in college. With $34 in his pocket when he arrived at NC A&T State University, Lee went job hunting as soon as he got settled in the dorm. His first job was a pot washer and Lee remembered not being allowed to enter the dining area because of his color.

It was while he was a student at NCA&TSU that he met his wife, Nancy, a student at Bennett College. Lee completed the electrical engineering courses at A&T in three years, volunteered for the navy, served two years, and came back to complete his degree on schedule.

Though well qualified, Lee was unable to obtain a job with any of the major companies in the Triad area because applications for employment were not accepted from blacks. He then took a teaching position at A&T and later decided to establish his own radio-television-electronics school in Winston-Salem. With the help of his attorney friend Curtiss Todd, Lee surmounted many obstacles and red tape, to open DelWatt's Radio and Electronics Institute in Winston-Salem.

Though he had about 300 students at DelWatt's at one time, Lee continued teaching at A&T and also opened the Ritz Theatre in Salisbury. Despite these accomplishments, Lee still felt somewhat unfulfilled. It was through his association with Todd and remembering past injustices suffered that ignited his interest in law.

There was no adequate place for blacks to study law locally. Lee reflected on the abundance of segregation and discrimination. He remembered the rampant discrimination he had witnessed in the Navy, his failure to receive a corporate job in electrical engineering due to his race, and many other obstacles he and his fellow brothers and sisters had experienced because of being black. All of this ignited an interest in him to get involved in the civil rights struggle.

It was around this time that a group of law students from NCCU in Durham had filed a lawsuit to be admitted to the law school at UNC-Chapel Hill. This lawsuit, McKissick vs. Carmichael, was being brought by the NAACP, but the plaintiffs would be graduating before a decision would be forthcoming. The NAACP had spent almost a quarter million dollars on the suit, and was now looking for someone else to take the departing students' place as plaintiff.

Thurgood Marshall was the attorney pressing the suit, along with several other prominent black attorneys. Lee talked with them and made the decision to intervene as plaintiff. The suit resulted in five black students, including Lee, enrolling in the school, marking the first time a black student attended public-supported classes with white students in the state of North Carolina.

"Two of the black students dropped out and one finished later, leaving Harvey Beech and I to experience life as the only two black law students at UNC Law School," explains Lee. "On our first day of enrollment, Harvey and I were stopped on the highway just outside Chapel Hill by a battery of highway patrolmen and news reporters. They escorted us onto campus and were our constant companions for the next several weeks."

Despite the backlog of applications which UNC-CH had always had, Lee recalls that Beech and himself were assigned an entire floor of a dormitory. Lee also recalls the first time he went to the dining hall to eat, escorted by two large armed highway patrolmen.

"There must have been five or six thousand students in there eating with the usual noise made by college students in the dining hall at mealtime. When I came through the door, with the escort, a deathly silence fell over the entire room and this was the first time I realized that my shoes squeaked," laughs Lee.

Lee remembers incidents such as being given football tickets for a section marked "colored." He protested, and received tickets with note attached encouraging him not to attend. But Lee says that not all of his fellow students harassed him. A day seldom went by without some type of incident, making it difficult to study, but there were still many decent white people on campus, Lee says. Despite all the problems, he finished law school in two and a half years, passing the bar prior to graduation.

Lee went on to become the assistant counsel for the NAACP, representing the organization in all civil rights cases in North Carolina. Lee was local counsel in the first suits brought in North Carolina to integrate public schools, swimming pools, golf courses, eating facilities and all other cases until the Sit In Demonstration of 1960. The suits Lee helped fight eventually resulted in desegregation of all public areas in the South.

"Representing criminal defendants in civil rights cases during these days was not easy and sometimes even dangerous, since the cases almost invariably involved alleged crimes by blacks against whites," says Lee.

During his tenure as a civil rights lawyer, he represented 33 defendants who were tried for their lives. Lee managed to keep every one from execution.

With the end of segregation and many other attorneys entering the civil rights arena, Lee decided to step down and consider areas of law that would permit him to improve the economic conditions of black people. Lee firmly believed that making money and doing good in the community were not necessarily inconsistent objectives.

Lee realized his calling when he was unable to obtain the money he needed from a local lending institution for a home he wanted, though he had good credit and had saved most of the money he needed. In 1957, it was the policy of all lending institutions in Guilford County to restrict loans for "colored" people no matter what the circumstance. Once again Lee encountered an obstacle that would influence the path of his career.

There were no black owned savings and loan associations in the state that were chartered by the federal government, and only one chartered by the state, Mutual Savings in Durham. Lee realized that white-owned lending institutions would set any limit they desired on blacks, and blacks had no choice but to accept it. So he set out to obtain a federal savings and loan charter.

After much hard work and with a great deal of help from colleagues, Lee successfully organized American Federal Savings and Loan Association. AFSLA opened its doors in March, 1959, with $350,000 in capital. It was the only federally chartered savings and loan in North Carolina.

For more than 33 years, Lee served as director, guiding the bank to a position of strength. At one time the bank's holdings totaled $25 million. AFSLA later merged with Mutual Savings Bank, where it continued to flourish.

Throughout his career, Lee was instrumental in changing conditions for black citizens for the better. He served on the North Carolina Housing and Finance Agency for 8 years, five of which as vice chairman. He was instrumental in getting 55,000 houses for low-income residents in North Carolina. He has also brokered multi-million dollar deals for apartment complexes, and also secured more than 17,000 apartments for low-income residents.

In 1992 Lee was inducted in the National Bar Association hall of Fame, conferred by President Clinton, for forty years of service. He also has received awards from Governor Hunt, the NAACP, Phi Beta Sigma, and many other civic organizations.

Lee now spends most of his time in leisure with his wife, Nancy. He and his wife had one son, Michael, who recently died of heart failure.

"The death of my son has been the hardest thing I've had to deal with since the death of my mother," Lee says. His mothers death was a hard blow, "but I've learned to live with it, just as I know, I'll learn to live with the death of my son. My son had three children, and I feel that my son lives on through my grandchildren."

J. Kenneth Lee learned early in life to accept the things he couldn't change, but he worked very hard to change the things he could. His dream today, after having seen so many come to life, is that young African Americans will appreciate and take advantage of the opportunities and freedoms that he, and others, fought so hard to achieve.

Time and Places for Relaxation

It is likely that readers, seeing a life so filled with efforts and accomplishments, might get the idea that J. Kenneth Lee's life was devoid of "good times." Nothing could be further from the truth--a truth, I hope that will be told one day in his biography. [This first effort to record **some** of the memorable moments of his life is **primarily just** that.]

High on Ken's list of "things" and places for fun and relaxation were golfing, hunting, fishing, entertaining, traveling, and weekly card-playing with his circle of buddies. Membership in organizations such as Kappa Alpha Psi Fraternity and the Guardsmen provided Ken and Nan with social outlets and Ken's shrewd investments in real estate kept all of us happily going to new places. For example, in 1979 when nine of the fourteen offshoots of the H. F. Lee family were still alive, Ken hosted a sibling reunion at his peaceful hide-away home on Lake Tillary in North Carolina. [The house was so hidden until finding it without a map became a family joke.] Michael claimed that he spent a night in his car within a few hundred feet from the house because he could not find the small road leading down to it. [My own stories of being left alone in the house, fully equipped by Ken, for work on the final stages of the FAMILY BOOK could easily be classified as mysteries if the truth were told.]

Family members who gathered for the 1979 "Sibling Reunion" at Tillary came to celebrate the 50th Wedding Anniversary of the oldest sister and her husband. Everyone received personal copies of "the Book": the honorees were presented a special golden-covered copy. It was a time of fellowship, love and pleasure--at Ken's expense, as were many other affairs for family and friends. Similar tales could be told by a lot of folks who spent happy times at Ken's expense (and pleasure) in all of his "get-away" places. Photos of three of his and Nan's favorite homes follow.

Final Confessions of The Editor-Ghostwriter

Near the end of Ken's chapter in the Family Book, he voiced this opinion: "My life has been, and is now, a rich and rewarding one." Reflecting on his life more than 30 years later he, nor anyone else, could argue with this assertion. There have, of course, been dark days--moments of agony, pain and great losses, none of which have been touted excessively in this volume. The choice has been ours--mine in deference to his desire for privacy and his because he sees obstacles not as deterrents but as stepping-stones. I think it is safe to say that he has successfully kept right on stepping.

He still lives in the house that "Hammer-the-Klansman" helped to build and upon completion declared a bomb or anything else would never hit it. [It never has been.] The house is full of gadgets [remnants of Ken's Electrical Engineering days and skills]. Lights go on and off, telephones take on peculiar characteristics, unexplainably loud voices announcing late night calls jar one awake etc.; the latter gadget is designed to lessen his hearing loss from a stroke suffered a few years ago. Through it all, he refuses to yield, as he refuses to be conquered by all other impediments. He still gets in his small sports car and moves through Greensboro, laughing as he goes [somewhat slower now] joking that people in Greensboro must surely think, "Lee has lost his mind."

On the outside doors of his house are carefully placed metal plates announcing the termination of his practice of law; this announcement frequently goes unheeded by those who still need his advice. Often he can be heard giving free counseling over one of his quirky phones or agreeing to meet somebody somewhere about something that needs solving. Perhaps all of this is still prompted by his memory of the admonition given him at Papa's graveside by one of Papa's close minister friends (see Lee's Chapter for details) on being held accountable for his acts--or more than likely from the lessons Papa and Mama drilled into all of us about "not hiding ones talent under a basket" and the "high expectations of those who are blessed with whatever." By precept and example, we learned and are still haunted by Papa's eyes and Mama's soft voice. [We all have much for which to be thankful!] Ken finds great satisfaction in "giving"--especially when the gift is bestowed unexpectedly; he also prefers to remain anonymous. [I can't resist relating one recent incident although I may get into trouble here.]

Not long ago a long-time minister friend and neighbor, The Rev. Dr. Howard A. Chubbs, added a beautiful community and family building to his church, Providence Baptist Church in Greensboro. This triggered Ken's memory of the significant history of the oldest Baptist church built for Blacks in the State (1866). [The historian in me demands that part of this story be told--not only as a special memory, but as black history.] The original church was organized under an arbor on land near East Market Street (later occupied by the massive Post Office Building). A frame building was constructed as a church and school in 1871 and replaced in 1876 by the first brick church building for Blacks in the state of North Carolina. It was razed in the 1960's to make way for urban renewal [a familiar story]. Having been involved with the legal side of much of this change, Ken was able to find a photograph of the early church before it was demolished in the name of progress. He had the battered photograph restored, enlarged and made into a magnificent rendering of the church, framed and presented to his minister friend for the new building named in honor of Rev. Chubbs [efforts at anonymity may have failed here]. With the restoration of the picture, Ken discovered that a car [He thinks an A Model Ford] was parked in front of the church and his curiosity almost took over his desire for anonymity. He decided to make a donation of $1,000 to the church in the name of anybody who could identify the owner of the car. To everyone's amazement, the widow of the car's owner claimed the honor, Mrs. Rosa Vines [still a faithful church member—thank Heaven for long-livers!]. [Some stories still have fairy-tale endings and prove that good deeds seldom go unrewarded.] The story did not end here, however. Another blessing occurred as Ken's rediscovery of Mrs. Vines brought back memories of his working with The Vines in their dry cleaning business when he was in school at A&T, serving at times as Mr.Vine's chauffer. [I added, probably **not** driving the car in the photo, however.]

This might also be a good time to give more thanks to Mama and Papa Lee "for bringing up a child in the way he should go." Other prominent family traits still surface in contacts with Ken; a sense of humor remains at the top of the list as illustrated throughout this writing and in our day-to-day preparation of this Memoir.

My time: Last week when sidetracked from this project by emergencies in my aging Kentucky community, I found myself offering apologies to Ken over the phone. In his usual manner, back came his humorous chuckle: "You just know too many old people." [Yeah, like you and me, maybe?] This was his compassionate, humorous way of recognizing my predicament and backing off while I dealt with my concerns. His remark kept churning around in my 4:30 a.m. sleepless brain, urging me to record right then some thoughts that could relate to this project. [Some just relate to me and how I got involved in this whole thing!]

In earlier days when research and scholarship mattered more to the "professional me" than it does now, I discovered that one of my favorite early black writers, Georgia Douglas Johnson, wore a small pad and pencil around her neck at all times because of her fear of losing a thought. I found that amusing in my youth; when I turned the corner at 80, it took on new meaning. Sister Lil, having turned the 80's corner 15 years ahead of me had a ready answer for me when I would ask why she was always up moving around in the middle of the night. Her answer for her sleepless nights: "Well the body is willing, but the mind just keeps on going." Indeed, my mind does keep racing on, but the thoughts rushing through it had better be grabbed and recorded fast or they may be gone by daylight. Both Ken and I have come to appreciate being the last of the PK's and the wisdom we inherited. We also are grateful for the "good genes" [must one say DNA now?] passed along that have permitted four of the fourteen siblings to still be alive as octogenarians; several others no longer with us also lived to be 80 and beyond.

Because of a sense of humor buried deep in our psyche, this final story from Ken's memory and an observation from his ghostwriter (or whatever) beg to end this book. Ken relates a memory of having been engaged in "lawyer research" in the dreary basement archives of the Yanceyville Courthouse [the town where our family started]. There, he swears, he found evidence of a family member being traded [in slavery] for a MULE. We then jokingly concluded that this could explain why there were so many "jackasses" in the family. Joke or no joke, mule or no mule our family stubbornness is surely reflected in Ken's willfulness and determination to succeed and open doors for others. His life is a reflection of his belief "that making money and doing good in the community [are] not necessarily inconsistent objectives."

The most public statement of this belief and of his determination to succeed is seen in his lifelong refusal to be run out of the South. NO WAY!

*****

The finding guides and inventories in the final section of this book are provided with the hope that future voices will be inspired to pick up the J. Kenneth Lee story and keep his legacy alive.

Winona Lee Fletcher

Part III
For Voices of The Future

J. KENNETH LEE
Attorney and Counsellor at Law
3011 East Market Street
Greensboro, North Carolina 27405

(919) 274-3749

Mailing Address
Post Office Box 20027
Greensboro, NC 27420

March 24, 1993

Dean Benjamin F. Speller, Jr.
Dean and Project Adminstrator
NC African American Archives Group
School of Library and Information
NC CENTRAL UNIVERSITY
Post Office Box 19586
Durham, NC 27707

Dear Dean Speller:

I have received your recent letter requesting documentary resources or information relating to African American History in North Carolina.

In the late 1940's, I was a student at NC Central, and a plaintiff in the lawsuit which resulted in the admission of Black students to the Law School at the University of NC at Chapel Hill. This was the first integration ever of students in State Schools in North Carolina.

I subsequently enrolled in the Law School under Federal Court Order and with the help of the State Highway Patrol, and was one of two students to graduate in the Law School class of 1952, the first year any Black students had received degrees from the University of North Carolina.

For the past 45 years or so, I have collected and retained documents which I felt would help Historians in the future to better understand the climate and the circumstances existing in the State during that period and perhaps better understand why the State expended so much energy and resources to win this case. My intent was to someday write a book about this subject with the use of the knowledge and materials available to me. However, I am now almost 70 years old, and with no experience in writing or publishing, it is beginning to look like the prospects of a book are more remote.

Some of the material I have, might possibly be obtained from other sources. These would include pleadings, etc. which were actually filed with the Court.

Sometime back, I checked with the Court Clerk and was advised

Dean Benjamin F. Speller, Jr.
Page 2
March 24, 1993

that they did not have these files in his office any longer.

It may be possible to reconstruct these records by getting them from various other sources like the Appeals Court, or lawyers involved in the case who might have retained records for 40 or 45 years, etc. However, even if this is done, I have serious doubts that the transcript of the actual testimony of all of the witnesses who testified would be available.

Also, transcripts of the Examinations and Cross Examinations of witnesses by Attorneys Thurgood Marshall, James Nabrit, Robert Carter, Spotswood Robinson and C. O. Pearson would give future generations a chance to see first hand how the greatest Black lawyers of this century successfully handled their cases.

I have all of this and many documents or copies of documents, receipts, letters, etc. which would not be available from any other source.

Most of the material I have are copies, since original documents are filed and left with the Court.

The material which I have, includes, but is not limited to the following:

(1) Complete transcript of witnesses testimony at trial.

(2) Letter from Henry Brandis, Jr. to me advising that Application for Admission to Law School has been approved and advising of terms of admission.

(3) Copy of telegram to Governor soliciting his aid when first Black students were assigned to the "Colored" section of the football stadium behind the goal posts.

(4) Docket sheet of U. S. District Court showing chronology of filing and all entries in the record from summons to judgment.

(5) Initial room assignment of Black students to room 33 in Steele dormitory - (only room assigned at that time - All other rooms in that section and on that floor left vacant).

Dean Benjamin F. Speller, Jr.
Page 3
March 24, 1993

(6) Student receipt #B-16098 for $6.00, the amount of room deposit required at that time. Receipt also shows no fees collected for other services such as swimming privileges, since we were not permitted to use swimming facilities, etc. at that time.

(7) Some interesting testimony of the views and attitudes of the time taken from such witnesses as:

  (a) Marshall T. Spears, Professor or Law at Duke University since 1927.
  (b) I. Beverly Lake, prominent segregationist of the time; and Professor of Law at Wake Forest; Dr. Lake's legal background included studies and degrees from Wake Forest, Harvard and Columbia. He is credited with being the force behind the founding of the Law School at Campbell.
  (c) Dr. Alphonso Elder - President, NC Central.
  (d) Fred B. McCall, Professor of Law at UNC and part-time Professor of Law at Central
  (e) Ervin N. Griswold, Dean, Harvard Law School
  (f) James M. Nabrit - Howard University Law School
  (g) Malcolm P. Sharp - University of Chicago Law School who was also a witness in the Sweat and Sipuel cases in Oklahoma.
  (h) Kingsland Van Winkle, a member of the Board of Examiners since one year after it was founded, testifying as to the equality of the two Law Schools.
  (i) George B. Greene, a charter member of the NC Board of Law Examiners and a practitioner since 1919 testifying that the Central Law School and students are in some ways superior to those at UNC notwithstanding that Central has no building or library.
  (j) John G. Herbey - Associate Dean of the Law School at Temple University and the Attorney for the Legal Education Section of the American Bar Association.
  (k) L. R. Varser, former Supreme Court Justice and Bar Examiner, who testified that since his admission to the NC Bar on October 1, 1901, he had never known of any Negro Lawyer who had represented a white client and had only heard of one such case this century. This, apparently,

Dean Benjamin F. Speller, Jr.
Page 4
March 24, 1993

      was the basis of the court's findings that Negroes
      had never represented whites in the state and that
      they should attend school where their clients would
      come from.
  (1) Some of the other witnesses subpoenaed included
      Dean Albert L. Turner, Mrs. Lucille Elliott and
      J. J. Sanson.

There are interesting historical facts contained in some of
the testimony which is not directly related to the issue of
segregation.

For instance, the testimony of Dean Brandis of the UNC Law
School reveals that the salaries for Professors and
Instructors at the Law School at UNC ranged from a low of
$4,500.00 per annum to $8,500.00 for the Dean, who received
$1,800.00 for serving as Dean and which was included in the
$8,500.00 annual salary. This can be compared to the
testimony of Miss Elliott, that the total annual budget for
the library at the Durham Law school was $24,323.00. This
included all salaries, books, binding and repairs, student
wages, librarian and assistants, etc.

(8) Copy of the Petition For a Writ of Certiorari to the
U. S. Court of Appeals for the Fourth Circuit from the Order
of the District Court denying relief.

(9) Order of the Court awarding the plaintiffs their cost in
the total amount of $493.00 after their successful appeal to
the Circuit Court.

(10) Copies of original summons, complaint, answers and
other routine legal documents filed during the course of the
litigation.

(11) 22 pages of most interesting findings of fact and
conclusions of law which formed the basis of the trial
court's determination that the Black students were not
discriminated against.

I also have one set of records which are not normally seen by
Historians nor contained in the public records. These are
the original handwritten notes made by the Presiding Judge

Dean Benjamin F. Speller, Jr.
Page 5
March 24, 1993

from the Bench during the course of the trial and used in instructing the Jury, when applicable, or as a basis of his findings of fact and conclusions when no jury is present, as in this case.

It would perhaps be interesting for Historians to read a transcript of the witness's testimony and compare it with the notes taken by the Presiding Judge at the time the testimony is being given.

The detailed and lengthy testimony of the Dean and Librarian at the UNC Law School described the conditions at the Law School in minute detail that could not begin to be understood by any one just reading the complaints, etc. filed with the Court, and I do not believe that these description could be found anywhere else. For instance, Dean Turner testifies that according to the N. C. C. records, the **entire Law School Plant** had a valuation of just $30,000.00. This was the amount the state had invested in the education of the Black lawyers.

The Attorneys representing the State and the University were the most prominent White Attorneys of that day, including two former Governors; their attitudes and lines of questioning reflect the attitude and policies of the State at that time and are interesting.

I have been approached with the idea of donating these records to be placed in the new Black History Building which is in the pre-construction stages on the campus of UNC. It is, after all, a part of UNC's history.

In my mind, it is also a part of the history of NC Central, since it all originated with the students of and on the campus of "NC College for Negroes".

This material also includes documents, materials, records and pictures of the first class of the Central Law School and its faculty; pictures of the classroom and the room used for a Library with the all the books stacked on the floor, etc.

My interest is in placing this material where it will be preserved, well organized and made available to the maximum number of interested people.

I have no interest in being paid any sum of money. I do,

Dean Benjamin F. Speller, Jr.
Page 6
March 24, 1993

however, believe the material to have a very substantial historic value and would expect the Donee to provide the proper appraisals and documentation to permit me to claim a tax deduction for the gift.

This letter is written simply to determine your interest in this material. It is not an offer to donate, but merely an invitation to discuss the matter further if this is the kind of material covered by your inquiry.

Please let me hear from you.

Sincerely,

J. Kenneth Lee

JKL:ghm

cc: Julius LeVonne Chambers, Chancellor
    NC Central University
    Mr. David Olson, State Archivist
    University of NC
    Mr. David Moltke-Hanson, Director
    Southern Historical Collection
    University of NC
    Ms. Linda Simmons Henry, Archivist
    NC Central University

Blind Copy

J. Kenneth Lee Papers Inventory (#4782)

Manuscripts Department, Library of the University of North Carolina at Chapel Hill

Collection Information

- Descriptive Summary Including Abstract
- Administrative Information
- Online Catalog Terms
- Biographical Note
- Collection Overview
- Organization of Collection
- Series Descriptions
- 1. UNC-CH Law School Legal Action, 1949-1994.
- 2. Biographical Information and Related Papers, 1950-1994.
- 3. Pictures, 1951-1974 and undated.

Contact Information:
Manuscripts Department
CB#3926, Wilson Library
University of North Carolina at Chapel Hill
Chapel Hill, NC 27514-8890
Phone: 919/962-1345
Fax: 919/962-3594
Email: mss@email.unc.edu
URL: http://www.lib.unc.edu/mss/

Processed by:
Tim Pyatt

Date Completed:
December 1995

Encoded by:
Lynn Pritcher

Descriptive Summary Including Abstract

Title
J. Kenneth Lee Papers 1949-1994
Creator
Lee, J. Kenneth (John Kenneth), 1923- .
Extent
About 120 items (1.5 linear feet).
Repository
Southern Historical Collection
Abstract
J. Kenneth Lee, lawyer of Greensboro, N.C., who became one of the first two African Americans to attend the University of North Carolina at Chapel Hill. Lee received his Juris Doctoris degree in 1952 and was subsequently involved in over 1,700 civil rights lawsuits during his 38 years of legal practice. Papers relate primarily to J. Kenneth Lee's lawsuit to attend the University of North at Chapel Hill's School of Law, where, in June 1951, he and Harvey Beech became the first African Americans to enroll after a lengthy lawsuit and appeal against the University. Included are copies of court papers, photographs of Beech and Lee registering and attending class, and copies of newspaper clippings describing the court battle and the University's reaction. Also included are some materials pertaining to the Law School at the North Carolina College at Durham (formerly the North Carolina College for Negroes and currently North Carolina Central University).

Administrative Information

Access
No restrictions.
Usage Restrictions
Copyright is retained by the authors of items in these papers, or their descendants, as stipulated by United States copyright law.
Provenance
Received from J. Kenneth Lee, Greensboro, N.C., 28 November 1995 (Acc. 95140).

Online Catalog Terms

Afro-American lawyers--North Carolina--History--20th century.
Afro-American universities and colleges--North Carolina.
Afro-Americans--Civil rights--North Carolina.
Afro-Americans--Education (Higher)--North Carolina.
Beech, Harvey E.
Civil rights--North Carolina--History--20th century.
College integration--North Carolina.
Education, Higher--North Carolina--History--20th century.
Law--Study and teaching--North Carolina--History--20th century.
Lawyers--North Carolina--History--20th century.
Lee, J. Kenneth (John Kenneth), 1923- .
North Carolina College at Durham. School of Law--History.
North Carolina--Race relations--20th century.
Segregation in higher education--North Carolina--History--20th century.
University of North Carolina (1793-1962). School of Law --History.
University of North Carolina at Chapel Hill--History--20th century.

Biographical Note

J. Kenneth Lee was born in Charlotte, N.C., on 1 November 1923, the thirteenth of fourteen children. Lee was graduated from Capital Highway High School in Hamlet, N.C., in 1941 with highest honors. He was graduated from North Carolina A & T with a degree in Electrical Engineering in 1945. He also served as electrician's mate, second class, in the Navy during World War II.
Lee became one of the first two African Americans to attend the University of North at Chapel Hill when he and Harvey Beech were admitted in June 1951 after a lengthy lawsuit and appeal against the University. They also were the first African American graduates from UNC when they received their Juris Doctoris degrees (formerly LL.B.) in 1952.
Lee was involved in over 1,700 civil rights lawsuits during his 38 years of legal practice. He was also founder, president, and chairman of American Federal Savings & Loan, the second African American-owned thrift in the state. Lee has served on the Barber Scotia College Board of Trustees and as a member of the North Carolina Banking Commission, the Minority Business Enterprise Advisory Board, the Commission on Human Relations (Greensboro, N.C.), and the National Bar Association Hall of Fame, among other public service and honorary positions.

Collection Overview

Papers relating primarily to J. Kenneth Lee's lawsuit to attend the University of North at Chapel Hill's School of Law. Included in Series 1 are copies of court papers and copies of newspaper clippings describing the court battle and the University's reaction. Also included are some materials pertaining to the Law School at the North Carolina College at Durham (formerly the North Carolina College for Negroes and currently North Carolina Central University). Series 2 contains biographical information. Photographs of Beech and Lee registering and attending class are located in Series 3.

Organization of Collection

1. UNC-CH Law School Legal Action
1.1. North Carolina College at Durham School of Law
1.2. Court Documents
1.3. UNC-CH Law School
2. Biographical Information & Related Papers
3. Pictures

Series Descriptions
1. UNC-CH Law School Legal Action, 1949-1994.

53 items.
These materials are divided into three groups: documents pertaining to the School of Law at the North Carolina College at Durham (formerly the North Carolina College for Negroes and currently North Carolina Central University); copies of the civil actions against the University of North Carolina requesting the right for African Americans to be admitted to the UNC-CH School of Law; and materials relating to the academic career of J. Kenneth Lee at UNC-CH.

1.1. North Carolina College at Durham. School of Law, 1950-1966.
3 items.
Pages 22-23 of the North Carolina College at Durham Law School yearbook for 1950, contain photographs and an account of the school's battle for accreditation, which is cited in the civil action court case.

Folder 1
North Carolina College at Durham transcript of J. Kenneth Lee

Folder 2
1950 Law School yearbook

Folder 3
Report: North Carolina College School of Law in the Context of Social Change (Dec. 1966)

1.2. Court Documents, 1949-1951.
About 30 items.
Primarily official photocopies of Civil Action No. 144, which was filed several times as the litigants changed and others were added to the case. The initial litigants were Harold Thomas Epps and Robert David Glass vs. William Donald Carmichael, Jr., President of the University of North Carolina, et al.

Folder 4
Complaint, filed 24 October 1949 (copy)

Folder 5
Civil Action no. 144, filed in U.S. District Court, 27 October 1949 (copy)

Folder 6
Civil Action no. 144, depositions of Henry Brandis, Jr., Lucille Elliott, and Albert Turner, 25 August 1950 (copy)

Folder 7
Civil Action no. 144, decree, filed 9 October 1950 (copy)

Folder 8-10
Civil Action no. 144, McKissick, Revis, Lassiter, and Lee vs. Carmichael, filed 27 November 1950 (copy)

Folder 11
McKissick, et al. vs. Carmicheal, Appeal no. 6201, filed in U.S. Court of Appeals, Fourth District, 27 November 1950 (copy)

Folder 12
McKissick, et al. vs. Carmicheal, Judgment, 26 September 1951

Folder 13-14
Documents pertaining to Civil Action no. 144

Folder 15
Copies of Judge Hayes' notes from Civil Action no.144

1.3. UNC-CH Law School, 1950-1994.
About 20 items.

Folder 16
Lee's UNC-CH career

Folder 17
Admission letter and diploma (copies)

2. Biographical Information and Related Papers, 1950-1994.

About 40 items.
Folder 18

Lee biographical material
Folder 19
Transcript of interview with Lee (from the Greensboro Public Library Oral History Program)
Folder 20
Correspondence with the North Carolina Department of Archives and History concerning use of Lee documents for an exhibit
Folder 21
Materials pertaining to establishing Harvey E. Beech Park in Kinston, N.C.
Folder 22
Materials pertaining to the 1990 Harvey E. Beech Award, given by UNC Black Alumni

3. Pictures, 1951-1974 and undated.

25 items.
P-4782-1: Photograph of Beech and Lee, first day of classes at UNC, 11 June 1951.
P-4782/2: Beech and Lee in Chancellor House's office.
P-4782/3: Beech and Lee complete registration, 11 June 1951.
P-4782/4: Lee, Beech, and other litigants.
P-4782/5: Lee being admitted to the North Carolina Bar.
P-4782/6: Lee as a young child.
P-4782/7: Lee in group photo.
P-4782/8: Lee with Horace Kornegay and others on the steps of the Supreme Court, May 1967.
P-4782/9: Lee making presentation to Theodore R. Bryant, North Carolina Central University Law School alumnus.
P-4782/10: North Carolina Minority Business Development Agency Board of Directors, 1973-74.
P-4782/11: American Federal Savings & Loan.
P-4782/12: Model for Beech park in Kinston, N.C. (Old Well at UNC-CH).
P-4782/13: Transparencies from presentation on Lee's admission to the UNC Law School.

As a public record, this finding aid of the J. Kenneth Lee Papers (#4782) is available at http//www.lib.unc.edu/mss/inv/l/Lee,J.Kenneth

J. KENNETH LEE COLLECTIONS

ICRCM 2004

	CATALOG ACRONYMS
AW	AWARDS
BO	BOOK / BOOKLETS
CD	COURT DOCUMENTS
CT	CASSETTE TAPES
HL	HAND WRITEN LETTERS
LA	LOAN APPLICATIONS
LD	LEGAL DOCUMENTS
M	MEDALS
NP	NEWS PAPER CLIPINGS
PH	PHOTOGRAPHY
PR	PROGRAMS
PQ	PLAQUES
TL	TYPED LETTERS
VHS	VIDEOS
YB	YEAR BOOKS
3D	THREE DIMENTIONAL OBJECTS

CATALOG NUMBER	ACCESSION NUMBER	DECRIPTION	HOW ACQUIRED	MUSEUM LOCATION
KL.1.2004.12.BO.1	Dec. 2004	Holy Ground – Significant events in the Civil Rights-related history of the African American communities of Guilford County, North Carolina, 1771-1995 By Hal Sieber	Gift	Archives
KL.1.2004.12.BO.2	Dec. 2004	LR Sixty Years- A look at L. Richardson Memorial Hospital 1921, written for the Greensboro Chapter of Links, Inc. By Shirley and Hal Sieber	Gift	Archives
		BOX 1-FOLDER1		
KL.1.2004.12.BO.3	Dec. 2004	A photographic History of Greensboro, North Carolina By Black artist	Gift	Archives
KL.1.2004.12.BO.4	Dec. 2004	Market Street Forum Exhibit '81 April 19- May 3, North Carolina A & T State University Gibbs Hall 123	Gift	Archives
KL.1.2004.12.BO.5	Dec. 2004	sauti mpya: Literary magazine of the Sonja Haynes Stone Black Cultural Center Vol.1, 2	Gift	Archives
KL.1.2004.12.BO.6	Dec. 2004	(4) Journey from Big Road: Lincoln Grove, A report to the Greensboro redevelopment commission, Greensboro City Council, United States Department of Housing and Urban Development, and the Lincoln Grove Community of the City of Greensboro	Gift	Archives
KL.1.2004.12.BO.7	Dec. 2004	A Vision Fulfilled: The bicentennial campaign for Carolina Office of Planned Giving	Gift	Archives
KL.1.2004.12.BO.8	Dec. 2004	American Federal Savings and Loan Association calendar 1989	Gift	Archives

CATALOG NUMBER	ACCESSION NUMBER	DECRIPTION	HOW ACQUIRED	MUSEUM LOCATION
KL.1.2004.12.BO.9	Dec. 2004	(6) 25 Years 1959-1984 The American Federal Story	Gift	Archives
KL.1.2004.12.BO.10	Dec. 2004	North Carolina Housing Finance Agency 1985 Annual Report	Gift	Archives
KL.1.2004.12.BO.11	Dec. 2004	North Carolina Housing Finance Agency 1986 Annual Report	Gift	Archives
KL.1.2004.12.BO.12	Dec. 2004	Premium rates for National Service Life Insurance and Total Disability Income Provisions	Gift	Archives
KL.1.2004.12.BO.13	Dec. 2004	Southern Legal History: A guide to holdings in the Southern Historical Collection, Southern Research Report, University of North Carolina at Chapel Hill	Gift	Archives
KL.1.2004.12.BO.14	Dec. 2004	(2) The Readers Digest First Person Series 2000 words "Strange Bedfellows" From the manuscript in preparation of H.F. Lee Family Book. Winona Lee Fletcher (Ghostwriter)	Gift	Archives
KL.1.2004.12.BO.15	Dec. 2004	The University of North Carolina at Chapel Hill: Office of Institutional Research "Fact Book" 1997-98	Gift	Archives
KL.1.2004.12.BO.16	Dec. 2004	"Home Work" A publication of The North Carolina Housing Finance Agency, Autumn 1985	Gift	Archives
KL.1.2004.12.BO.17	Dec. 2004	"Winning Some Battles but Losing the War? Black and Urban Renewal in Greensboro, NC., 1953-1965 By Sigmund C. Shipp, Asst. Professor, Hunter Collage Department of Urban Affairs and Planning, New York, NYC	Gift	Archives

CATALOG NUMBER	ACCESSION NUMBER	DECRIPTION	HOW ACQUIRED	MUSEUM LOCATION
KL.1.2004.12.BO.18	Dec. 2004	Law School Association and North Carolina Law Review	Gift	Archives
KL.1.2004.12.CD.1	Dec. 2004	State vs. Phillip Cooke ET AL Defendants exhibit #1 1946 Guilford County, North Carolina and Gillespie Park Golf Course.	Gift	**Courts and the Quest for Justice**
		Charge of the court – judgment ect.		
KL.1.2004.12.CD.2	Dec. 2004	State vs. Phillip Cooke ET AL 1956 List of State witnesses, State rest, amendments to warrant Motion of non-suit, stipulation as to possession, Charge of the court	Gift	**Courts and the Quest for Justice**
KL.1.2004.12.CT.1	Dec. 2004	Southern Oral History Program School of Law Oral History ProjectInt. With J. Kenneth Lee October 26, 1995 By Ann Estridge Cassettes 1-4	Gift	Archives
KL.1.2004.12.LA.1	Dec. 2004	1967 original loan application for Cumberland Shopping Center	Gift	Archives
KL.1.2004.12.LA.2-3	Dec. 2004	1984 appendices and exhibits for Greensboro urban development Action grant for Lincoln Grove Shopping Center.	Gift	Archives

CATALOG NUMBER	ACCESSION NUMBER	DECRIPTION	HOW ACQUIRED	MUSEUM LOCATION
		FOLDER 2		
KL.1.2004.12.LD.1	Dec. 2004	Articles of Amendment of North Carolina A&T State University Alumni Association, Inc. Jan.7, 1971 (copy)	Gift	Archives
KL.1.2004.12.LD.2	Dec. 2004	Articles of Amendment of North Carolina A&T State University Alumni Association, Inc. Nonprofit Corporation June 22 1999 (copy)	Gift	Archives
KL.1.2004.12.LD.3	Dec. 2004	Articles of Incorporation of North Carolina A&T State University State University Alumni Association, Inc. Certificate of Incorporation #70589 (copy)	Gift	Archives
KL.1.2004.12.LD.4	Dec. 2004	Dimensional information for Lee family home in Pinehurst Southern Pines MLS	Gift	Archives
KL.1.2004.12.LD.5	Dec. 2004	J. Kenneth Lee's University of North Carolina Chapel Hill Student Room Deposit Receipt No. B-1 6098 Aug. 31, 1951 $6.00, Room No. 33 in Steele Dormitory, June 12 1951	Gift	Archives
KL.1.2004.12.LD.6	Dec. 2004	J. Kenneth Lee announcement card of his new office at 914 Gorrell St. Greensboro, N.C.	Gift	Archives
KL.1.2004.12.LD.7	Dec. 2004	Feb.1, 1944 Notice of Classification card, Local Board No.2 Guilford County, Greensboro, N.C.	Gift	Archives
KL.1.2004.12.LD.8	Dec. 2004	Nursing Home Administration Certificate No. 095, Sep.19, 1983	Gift	Archives
KL.1.2004.12.LD.9	Dec. 2004	State of North Carolina Department of the Secretary of State, Raleigh, Member of North Carolina Banking Commission card, Aug. 17, 1973	Gift	

CATALOG NUMBER	ACCESSION NUMBER	DESCRIPTION	HOW ACQUIRED	MUSEUM LOCATION
		FOLDER 2		
KL.1.2004.12.LD.10	**Dec. 2004**	State of North Carolina Department of the Secretary of State, Raleigh, Member of the North Carolina Housing Finance Agency Board of Directors card, Mar. 17, 1988	Gift	Archives
KL.1.2004.12.LD.11	**Dec. 2004**	Modification and renewal of note and extension of real estate lien for property located at 900 E. Lee St. and 703-705 Reid St. Greensboro, N.C., Jul. 17, 1992	Gift	Archives
KL.1.2004.12.LD.12	**Dec. 2004**	Copy of first payment receipt for the first loan made by American Federal (No. 6-1) $50.25 from Charles Ruffin, Jr.	**Gift**	Archives
KL.1.2004.12.LD.13	**Dec. 2004**	Law Alumni Reception and Banquet registration receipt, Aug 13, 1998	Gift	Archives
KL.1.2004.12.LD.14	**Dec. 2004**	United States of America State of North Carolina, North Carolina Housing Finance Agency: Single Family, Multi-Family Revenue Bond, Series C, E (1985 Resolution) sample	Gift	Archives
		FOLDER 3		
KL.1.2004.12.NP.1	**Dec. 2004**	Sunday, Aug. 18, 1963 Greensboro Daily News: 170 Candidates Pass State Bar Examination – Alvis Augustus Lee, Greensboro	Gift	Archives
KL.1.2004.12.NP.2	**Dec. 2004**	Friday, Apr. 5, 1968 Greensboro Daily News: Incidents of violence flare across nation, 300 Negroes March here; windows smashed	Gift	Archives

CATALOG NUMBER	ACCESSION NUMBER	DECRIPTION	HOW ACQUIRED	MUSEUM LOCATION
		FOLDER 3		
KL.1.2004.12.NP.3	Dec. 2004	Sunday, Feb. 22, 1970 Greensboro Daily News: Visiting Negroes see city as it is	Gift	Archives
KL.1.2004.12.NP.4	Dec. 2004	Saturday, May 5, 1984 Carolina Peacemaker: A&T Confers Two Honorary Degrees on Sunday J. Kenneth Lee, and Obrie Smith Jr.	Gift	Archives
KL.1.2004.12.NP.5	Dec. 2004	Saturday, Jul. 28, 1984 Carolina Peacemaker: American Federals Jubilee Celebration – J. Kenneth Lee accepting Order of the Long Leaf Pine award from Alexander Killens	Gift	Archives
KL.1.2004.12.NP.6	Dec. 2004	Tuesday, Mar. 12, 1985: Junior Achievement to induct 3 into Business Leaders Hall- Lee, Myers, Boren	Gift	Archives
KL.1.2004.12.NP.7	Dec. 2004	Saturday, Feb 22, 1986 Carolina Peacemaker: Local black financial institutions products of vision and sound business practices	Gift	Archives
KL.1.2004.12.NP.8	Dec. 2004	Tuesday, Jun.30, 1987 Greensboro News & Record: Retiring executive gets thank from many (A.S. Webb)	Gift	Archives
KL.1.2004.12.NP.9	Dec. 2004	Saturday, Jun 17, 1989 Carolina Peacemaker: B.J. Battle heads local S&L Association	Gift	Archives
KL.1.2004.12.NP.10	Dec. 2004	Monday, Oct. 23, 1989 Greensboro News & Record: Profile J. Kenneth Lee "A place in history"	Gift	Archives

CATALOG NUMBER	ACCESSION NUMBER	DECRIPTION	HOW ACQUIRED	MUSEUM LOCATION
		FOLDER 3		
KL.1.2004.12.NP.11	Dec. 2004	Saturday, Jul. 8, 1989 Carolina Peacemaker: Greensboro 100 Two men have significant influence, J. Kenneth Lee, Robert J. Brown	Gift	Archives
KL.1.2004.12.NP.12	Dec. 2004	Sunday, Sept. 23, 1990 Greensboro News & Record Centennial Edition II	Gift	Archives
KL.1.2004.12.NP.13	Dec. 2004	Sunday, Nov. 11, 1990 News and Observer: Taking stock after a hard fight, Jesse A. Helms v Harvey B. Gantt	Gift	Archives
KL.1.2004.12.NP.14	Dec. 2004	Wednesday, Apr. 22, 1993 Carolina Peacemaker: Dr. Gibbs, President of NCA&TSU 1955 " We teach our students how to think, not what to think." Dies at 101	Gift	Archives
KL.1.2004.12.NP.15	Dec. 2004	Thursday, Feb. 8 thru 14, 1996 Carolina Peacemaker: Sit-In Breakfast evokes memories, J. Kenneth Lee: Adversity Lesson	Gift	Archives
KL.1.2004.12.NP.16	Dec. 2004	Thursday, Mar. 28, 2001 Carolina Peacemaker: United Health Care add of Lee with his wife Nancy Lee	Gift	Archives
KL.1.2004.12.NP.17	Dec. 2004	March 24, 2002 News & Record: The Power of One "Man undeterred by the system stacked against him. J. Kenneth Lee: Dismantling the walls of prejudice	Gift	Archives
KL.1.2004.12.NP.18	Dec. 2004	Thursday, Apr. 18, 2002 The Greensboro Times: Black Wall Street and the East Market Street Corridor	Gift	Archives

CATALOG NUMBER	ACCESSION NUMBER	DECRIPTION	HOW ACQUIRED	MUSEUM LOCATION
		FOLDER 3		
KL.1.2004.12.NP.19	Dec. 2004	Sunday, May 9, 2004 Los Angeles Times: For Civil Rights Pioneer a life of quiet struggle: Josephine Boyd	Gift	Archives
KL.1.2004.12.NP.20	Dec. 2004	Carolina Peacemaker special: Lawyer describes friendship with Klansman	Gift	Archives
KL.1.2004.12.NP.21	Dec. 2004	David Richmond, sit-in leader dies BY Bernie Woodall	Gift	Archives
KL.1.2004.12.NP.22	Dec. 2004	News & Record "Pitch a Boogie Woogie" Restored all-black film is a historic treasure	Gift	Archives
		BINDER 1		
KL.1.2004.12.AW.1	Dec. 2004	City of Greensboro Human Relations Commission in recognition of it's Twenty-Fifth Anniversary (1963-1988) for outstanding service on the Commission	Gift	Archives
KL.1.2004.12.AW.2	Dec. 2004	February One Society - One Community Award 1960-1985 for contribution to the community	Gift	Archives
KL.1.2004.12.AW.3	Dec. 2004	North Carolina Council of Women certificate of appreciation March 25, 1992	Gift	Archives
KL.1.2004.12.AW.4	Dec. 2004	State of North Carolina appointment as Vice-Chairman of the North Carolina Housing Finance Agency Board of Directors. February 12, 1988, James G. Martin, Governor	Gift	Archives
KL.1.2004.12.AW.5	Dec. 2004	State of North Carolina appointment as Vice-Chairman of the North Carolina Housing Finance Agency Board of Directors. July 1, 1989, James G. Martin, Governor	Gift	Archives

CATALOG NUMBER	ACCESSION NUMBER	DECRIPTION	HOW ACQUIRED	MUSEUM LOCATION
		BINDER 1		
KL.1.2004.12.AW.6	Dec. 2004	Resolution expressing appreciation for service to the North Carolina Housing Finance Agency Board of Directors Resolution 93-85 December 9, 1993, Lucius Jones, Chairman	Gift	Archives
KL.1.2004.12.AW.7	Dec. 2004	American Federal Savings and Loan Association of Greensboro Charter Certificate June 30, 1959	Gift	Archives
KL.1.2004.12.AW.8	Dec. 2004	Federal Savings and Loan Insurance Corporation Certificate of Insurance No.4255 That AFSLAG has become a insured institution June 3, 1959	Gift	Archives
KL.1.2004.12.AW.9	Dec. 2004	Official thanks and letter of appreciation for service in the Armed Forces of the U.S.A.The White House	Gift	Archives
KL.1.2004.12.AW.10	Dec. 2004	Certificate of Membership to The National Bar Association 1992-1993	Gift	Archives
KL.1.2004.12.AW.11	Dec. 2004	North Carolina State Bar Certificate of Appreciation for Fifth Years or More of Service October 17, 2002	Gift	Archives
KL.1.2004.12.AW.12	Dec. 2004	North Carolina A&T State University Citation for distinguished service and leadership May5, 1974	Gift	Archives

CATALOG NUMBER	ACCESSION NUMBER	DECRIPTION	HOW ACQUIRED	MUSEUM LOCATION
		BINDER 1		
KL.1.2004.12.PH.1	Dec. 2004	B/W photo of 20th annual award banquet, Capitol Press Club, Washington Dc. May 18 1963. John Winters, Dr John Larkins, US Sen. Terry Sanford and J. Kenneth Lee.	Gift	Archives
KL.1.2004.12.PH.2	Dec. 2004	B/W portrait of J. Kenneth Lee when he arrived at North Carolina A&T University	Gift	Archives
KL.1.2004.12.PH.3	Dec. 2004	B/W group photo (including Lee) of Black lawyers practicing in North Carolina	Gift	Archives
KL. 1.2004.12.PH.4	Dec. 2004	B/W group photo of J. Kenneth Lee, Harvey Beech, and Jim Lassiter, Chancellor of UNC Chapel Hill First meeting prior to registration at the Univ.	Gift	Archives
KL.1.2004.12.PH.5	Dec. 2004	B/W photo J. Kenneth Lee, Jim Lassiter, Harvey Beech registering at UNC Chapel Hill	Gift	Archives
KL.1.2004.12.PH.6	Dec. 2004	B/W photo Harvey Beech, Jim Lassiter, J. Kenneth Lee getting dorm room assignments at UNCCH	Gift	Archives
KL.1.2004.12.PH.7	Dec. 2004	B/W photo of Harvey Beech, Jim Lassiter, J. Kenneth Lee coming out of Steel dorm UNC Chapel Hill where they had the top floor	Gift	Archives
KL.1.2004.12.PH.8	Dec. 2004	B/W photo Harvey Beech, J. Kenneth Lee, Jim Lassiter by the old well UNC Chapel Hill	Gift	Archives

CATALOG NUMBER	ACCESSION NUMBER	DECRIPTION	HOW ACQUIRED	MUSEUM LOCATION
		BINDER 1		
KL.1.2004.12.PH.9	Dec. 2004	38 color 35mm print photos of Nov. 3, 1979 Funeral march for six communist workers party members killed in shootout, east Market St. Greensboro, NC	Gift	Archives
KL.1.2004.12.PH.10	Dec. 2004	12 color 35mm color prints J. Kenneth Lee receiving Hon. Doctor of Law Degree, North Carolina A&T State Univ.	Gift	Archives
KL.1.2004.12.PH.11	Dec. 2004	Color photograph of "Montel Works" store front	Gift	Archives
KL.1.2004.12.PH.12	Dec. 2004	J. Kenneth Lee home at Pinehurst, view from Golf Course	Gift	Archives
KL.1.2004.12.PH.13	Dec. 2004	J. Kenneth Lee at home with wife Mrs. Nancy Young Lee	Gift	Archives
KL.1.2004.12.PH.14	Dec. 2004	J. Kenneth Lee's sister (Polly) in front of gazebo and Cadillac	Gift	Archives
KL. 1.2004.12.PH.15	Dec. 2004	Four color printed copies of J. Kenneth Lee at family home on Topside Island	Gift	Archives
KL.1.2004.12.PH.16	Dec. 2004	11x17 color copy of Lee family home in Pinehurst	Gift	Archives
KL.1.2004.12.PH.17	Dec. 2004	J. Kenneth Lee and Mrs. Nancy Young Lee at award banquet	Gift	Archives
KL.1.2004.12.PH.18	Dec. 2004	Mrs. Nancy Young Lee at award banquet group photograph	Gift	Archives

CATALOG NUMBER	ACCESSION NUMBER	DECRIPTION	HOW ACQUIRED	MUSEUM LOCATION
		BOX 2-FOLDER 4a, 4b		
KL.1.2004.12.PR.1	Dec. 2004	Service of Open House: American Federal Savings and Loan Association of Greensboro June 26, 1959	Gift	Archives
KL.1.2004.12.PR.2	Dec. 2004	Service of Open House: American Federal Savings and Loan Association of Greensboro June 24, 1971 (hand written notes)	Gift	Archives
KL.1.2004.12.PR.3	Dec. 2004	Memorial Service for Mrs. Zoe Parks Barbee: Sunday, Dec. 29, 1974 Harrison Auditorium NCA&TSU Reverend Earl Wilson, Jr. Pastor of Laughlin Memorial United Methodist Church	Gift	Archives
KL.1.2004.12.PR.4	Dec. 2004	North Carolina A&T State University 84th Annual Commencement: Sunday, May4, 1975 Greensboro Coliseum	Gift	Archives
KL.1.2004.12.PR.5	Dec. 2004	North Carolina Association of Black Lawyers: Pioneer Black Lawyers Award Banquet, March27, 1981 North Carolina Central University School of Law, Durham, North Carolina	Gift	Archives
KL.1.2004.12.PR.6	Dec. 2004	The Fifth Annual Greensboro Business Leaders Hall of Fame Awards Luncheon: Wednesday, March 14, 1984 Starmount Forest Country Club	Gift	Archives
KL.1.2004.12.PR.7	Dec. 2004	(5) Silver Jubilee Twenty-Fifth Anniversary Celebration: American Federal Savings and Loan Association of Greensboro	Gift	Archives

CATALOG NUMBER	ACCESSION NUMBER	DECRIPTION	HOW ACQUIRED	MUSEUM LOCATION
KL.1.2004.12.PR.8	**Dec. 2004**	N.C. Association of Black Lawyers Second Pioneer Black Lawyers Award Banquet, Oct. 26, 1984 NCCU Durham, North Carolina	Gift	Archives
		BOX 2-FOLDER 4a, 4b		
KL.1.2004.12.PR.9	**Dec. 2004**	(5) Sixth Annual Greensboro Business Leaders Hall of Fame Awards Luncheon: Wednesday, March 13, 1985 Starmount Forest Country Club	Gift	Archives
KL.1.2004.12.PR.10	**Dec. 2004**	Ceremony of Dedication: Bennett Collage Alumnae House Friday, May 8th, 1987 Mary Thrift Coleman presiding	Gift	Archives
KL.1.2004.12.PR.11	**Dec. 2004**	The Unveiling Ceremony of the statue of Ronald E. McNair June 12, 1987	Gift	Archives
KL.1.2004.12.PR.12	**Dec. 2004**	Fiftieth Wedding Anniversary 1944-1994 Kenneth & Nancy Lee	Gift	Archives
KL.1.2004.12.PR.13	**Dec. 2004**	Twenty-Fifth Anniversary GALA V February One Society, Inc.	Gift	Archives
KL.1.2004.12.PR.14	**Dec. 2004**	National Bar Association Annual Awards Banquet, Friday, July 31, 1992	Gift	Archives
KL.1.2004.12.PR.15	**Dec. 2004**	Groundbreaking Ceremony Dudley-Lee Complex, April 6, 2001 Greensboro, NC	Gift	Archives
KL.1.2004.12.PR.16.	**Dec. 2004**	Groundbreaking Ceremony Hayes-Taylor Memorial Branch YMCA, October 26, 1986	Gift	Archives
KL.1.2004.12.TS.1	**Dec. 2004**	1995 Interview with John Kenneth Lee School of Law oral history project Univ. NC at Chapel Hill	Gift	Archives

CATALOG NUMBER	ACCESSION NUMBER	DECRIPTION	HOW ACQUIRED	MUSEUM LOCATION
		BOX 2-FOLDER 5		
KL.1.2004.12.TL.1	Dec. 2004	September 2, 1946 Western Union telegram to J. Kenneth Lee from Alvis offering him a position for "Lectrical Instructor 200.00 per month with possible raise of 25.00	Gift	Archives
KL.1.2004.12.TL.2	Dec. 2004	J. Kenneth Lee Transcript from Capital Highway High School, Hamlet, N.C. 10/9/1937-5/30/1941	Gift	Archives
KL.1.2004.12.TL.3	Dec. 2004	July 29, 1944 letter of recommendation from A.C. Bowling Head, Electrical Eng. Dept. North Carolina A&T State University	Gift	Archives
KL.1.2004.12.TL.4	Dec. 2004	August 5, 1944 letter of recommendation from J.W. Mask, Jr. Principal of Capital Highway High School, Hamlet, North Carolina	Gift	Archives
KL.1.2004.12.TL.5	Dec. 2004	July 28, 1944 letter of recommendation from N.C. Webster, Bursar of A&T State University and owner of Triangle News and Smoke Shop	Gift	Archives
KL.1.2004.12.TL.6	Dec. 2004	July 28, 1944 letter of recommendation from N.C. Webster	Gift	Archives

CATALOG NUMBER	ACCESSION NUMBER	DECRIPTION	HOW ACQUIRED	MUSEUM LOCATION
		BOX 2-FOLDER 5		
KL.1.2004.12.TL.7	**Dec. 2004**	August 4, 1944 letter of recommendation from Warmoth T. Gibbs, Dean of North Carolina A&T State University	Gift	Archives
KL.1.2004.12.TL.8	**Dec. 2004**	J. Kenneth Lee employment application to Western Electric Company June 3, 1946	Gift	Archives
KL.1.2004.12.TL.9	**Dec. 2004**	August 4, 1944 letter of recommendation from North Carolina A&T State University Commanding Officer, Navel Training Program, Warmoth T. Gibbs	Gift	Archives
KL.1.2004.12.TL.10	**Dec. 2004**	August 7, 1944 letter of recommendation from C.T. Cartwright, Recruit Training Command, U.S. Navel Training Center Great Lakes, Illinois	Gift	Archives
KL.1.2004.12.TL.11	**Dec. 2004**	August 15, 1946 Norfolk Virginia, Federal Communications Commission, Restricted Radio Telephone Operator Permit	Gift	Archives
KL.1.2004.12.TL.12	**Dec. 2004**	United States Of America Veterans Administration Certificate of Eligibility February 6, 1947 Loan Guarantee Division, Charlotte, N.C.	Gift	Archives
KL.1.2004.12.TL.13	**Dec. 2004**	May 20, 1958 Federal Home Loan Bank Board No.11, 632 By Harry W. Caulsen, Secretary. Notice of hearing held in Washington D.C. Dec23, 1957 for permission to organize a Federal Savings and Loan Association located in Greensboro, N.C.	Gift	Archives

CATALOG NUMBER	ACCESSION NUMBER	DECRIPTION	HOW ACQUIRED	MUSEUM LOCATION
		BOX 2-FOLDER 5		
KL.1.2004.12.TL.15	Dec. 2004	November 13, 1968 correspondence letters from Horace R. Kornegay Congress of The United States House of Representatives, Washington, D.C and J.C. Berriman, Captain, U.S. Navy Director of Transportation in response to J. Kenneth Lee's request to visit his son and daughter in law at Guantanamo Bay	Gift	Archives
KL.1.2004.12.TL.16	Dec. 2004	November 14, 1968 approval letter for J. Kenneth Lee and Nancy Lee from E.D. Murphy Deputy Director Personnel Transportation Division, Department of the Navy, Bureau of Navel Personnel, Washington, D.C. to enter Guantanamo Bay Cuba December 20, 1968	Gift	Archives
KL.1.2004.12.TL.17	Dec. 2004	October 20, 1969 approval letter and boarding pass from E.D. Murphy Deputy Director Personnel Transportation, Department of the Navy, Bureau of Navel Personnel, Washington D.C. for J. Kenneth Lee and Nancy Lee to enter Guantanamo Bay Cuba October 30, 1969	Gift	Archives
KL.1.2004.12.TL.18	Dec. 2004	April 19, 1984 Congratulatory letter and program from Edward B. Fort, Chancellor North Carolina A&T State University for his Honorary Degree of Doctor Of Law to be conferred at 1984 Commencement May6, 1984	Gift	Archives

No Way!

CATALOG NUMBER	ACCESSION NUMBER	DECRIPTION	HOW ACQUIRED	MUSEUM LOCATION
		BOX 2-FOLDER 5		
KL.1.2004.12.TL.19	Dec. 2004	September 26, 1984 Thank you letter from Sampson Buie, Jr. Director-Office of Alumni Affairs North Carolina A&T State University	Gift	Archives
KL.1.2004.12.TL.20	Dec. 2004	January 28, 1985 Congratulations for being selected to the Greensboro Business Leader Hall of Fame. From Gail B. Drake, NCNB National Bank Greensboro, NC	Gift	Archives
KL.1.2004.12.TL.21	Dec. 2004	March 12, 1985 Hall of Fame congratulations letter from Robert S. Chiles, Sr. President of Greensboro National Bank	Gift	Archives
KL.1.2004.12.TL.22	Dec. 2004	March 4, 1987 Thank you letter from Lanette Renee Smith, Bennett Collage Class of '87 for his gift of $22,000 to refurbish the home of Dr. and Mrs. David D. Jones now know as the Alumnae House	Gift	Archives
KL.1.2004.12.TL.23	Dec. 2004	April 23, 1987 letter from Gladys Ashe Robinson President Bennett Collage, to confirm J. Kenneth Lee's participation in dedication ceremonies of Alumnae House Friday, May 8,???_?	Gift	Archives
KL.1.2004.12.TL.24	Dec. 2004	September 21, 1987 from J. Kenneth Lee to all employees of American Federal Savings and Loan Association enter office memorandum regarding operation adjustments (see attached chart)	Gift	Archives

CATALOG NUMBER	ACCESSION NUMBER	DECRIPTION	HOW ACQUIRED	MUSEUM LOCATION
		BOX 2-FOLDER 5		
KL.1.2004.12.TL.25	Dec. 2004	November 23 1987 Letter to the Board of Directors of American Federal Savings &Loan Association announcing J. Kenneth Lee's resignation after 33 years.	Gift	Archives
KL.1.2004.12.TL.26	Dec. 2004	January 7, 1988 Signed agreement letter by Board Members accepting Lee's resignation and advancing his status to Emeritus with all rights and privileges attached	Gift	Archives
KL.1.2004.12.TL.27	Dec. 2004	February 12, 1988 from North Carolina Governor James G. Martin appointing J. Kenneth Lee Vice-Chairman of the North Carolina Housing Finance Agency Board of Directors	Gift	Archives
KL.1.2004.12.TL.28	Dec. 2004	July 13, 1988 American Federal Savings and Loan Association of Greensboro's 29th Annual Shareholders Meeting reading of affidavits	Gift	Archives
KL.1.2004.12.TL.29	Dec. 2004	October 1, 1992 from North Carolina Governor James G. Martin thanking J. Kenneth Lee for his service and commending him on his accomplishments with the North Carolina Housing Finance Agency Board	Gift	Archives

CATALOG NUMBER	ACCESSION NUMBER	DECRIPTION	HOW ACQUIRED	MUSEUM LOCATION
		BOX 2-FOLDER 5		
KL.1.2004.12.TL.30	Dec. 2004	(3copies) March 24, 1993 letter to Benjamin F. Speller, Jr. Dean and Project Administrator NC African American Archives Group School of Library and Information North Carolina Central University, Durham, N.C. informing Mr. Lee of various copies that may be available to his organization i.e. Witness's testimony, Docket sheet of U.S. District court, student receipt for dorm room, swimming privileges, ect.	Gift	Archives
KL.1.2004.12.TL.31	Dec. 2004	April 5, 1993 from North Carolina Central University Chancellor Julius L. Chambers informing him that they are indeed interested in collecting materials described in a previous letter.	Gift	Archives
KL.1.2004.12.TL.32	Dec. 2004	May 3, 1993 from North Carolina Central University, Dean Benjamin F. Speller, Jr. Thanking Mr. Lee for detailed description of records related to the Civil Rights.	Gift	Archives
KL.1.2004.12.TL.33	Dec. 2004	November 2, 1995 from The University of North Carolina Chapel Hill Director, Special Campaigns Marjorie L. Corwell thanking him for attending the reception for the Sonja Haynes Stone Black Culture Center November 12th	Gift	Archives

CATALOG NUMBER	ACCESSION NUMBER	DECRIPTION	HOW ACQUIRED	MUSEUM LOCATION
		BOX 2-FOLDER 5		
KL.1.2004.12.TL.34	Dec. 2004	November 14, 1995 from The University of North Carolina at Chapel Hill, Director Special Campaigns, Marjorie L. Crowell thanking him for his generous gift of $1,000. For the Sonja Haynes Stone Black Cultural Center	Gift	Archives
KL.1.2004.12.TL.35	Dec. 2004	December 12, 1995 letter and initial inventory (#4782) from Timothy D. Pyatt, Assistant Curator of Manuscripts for The University of North Carolina At Chapel Hill for papers donated in November 1995	Gift	Archives
KL.1.2004.12.TL.36	Dec. 2004	May 29, 1998 from University of North Carolina at Chapel Hill School of Law, Director, Annual Fund and Alumni Affairs, Sheryl L. Aikman, congratulating J. Kenneth Lee as a recipient of UNC Law School Distinguished Alumni Awards	Gift	Archives
Kl.1.2004.12.TL.37	Dec. 2004	June 4, 1998 from University of North Carolina at Chapel Hill, Judith W. Wegner, Dean and Professor of Law thanking J. Kenneth Lee for his gift of $200.00 for the Law Annual Fund	Gift	Archives
KL.1.2004.12.TL.38	Dec. 2004	June 24, 1998 from University of North Carolina at Chapel Hill School of Law, Dean and Professor of Law Judith W. Wegner congratulating J. Kenneth Lee for his being honored as one of the 1998 Distinguished Law Alumni	Gift	Archives

CATALOG NUMBER	ACCESSION NUMBER	DECRIPTION	HOW ACQUIRED	MUSEUM LOCATION
		BOX 2-FOLDER 5		
KL.1.2004.12.TL.39	Dec. 2004	March 19, 1999 from University of North Carolina at Chapel Hill, Laura Y. Baxley, Assistant to the Keeper, North Carolina Collection Gallery requesting to interview Mr. Lee for a research project on Civil Right in Greensboro, N.C.	Gift	Archives
KL.1.2001.12.TL.40	Dec. 2004	April 8, 1999 response letter from J. Kenneth Lee to Laura Y. Baxley, informing her that he would be happy to grant her request for an interview for her research at UNCCH	Gift	Archives
KL.1.2004.12.TL.41	Dec. 2004	April 21, 1999 thank you letter from Laura Y. Baxley Assistant to the Keeper, North Carolina Collection Gallery, The University of North Carolina Chapel Hill	Gift	Archives
KL.1.2004.12.TL.42	Dec. 2004	June 7, 1999 from General Alumni Association Chairman Rodney Harris and Larry LaRusso, Coordinator of Extended Study, inviting Mr. Lee to speak at 15th Annual UNC Black Alumni Reunion	Gift	Archives
KL.1.2004.12.TL.43	Dec. 2004	April 1, 2001 from North Carolina A&T State University, Vice Chancellor for Academic Affairs, Carolyn W. Meyers congratulating him for being named Carolina Peacemaker's "Exceptional Person of the Month".	Gift	Archives

KL.1.2004.12.TL.44	**Dec. 2004**	December 7, 2001 introductory letter to David Hoard, C.E.O Sit-In Movement, Inc. informing him of his willingness to assist the museum in it's fundraising efforts. Suggesting that donating original documents could be appraised to assist in this effort	Gift	Archives
KL.1.2004.12.TL.45	**Dec. 2004**	January 29, 2003 Letter from The North Carolina State Bar informing J. Kenneth Lee that his petition for inactive status was granted on Jan 24, 2003	Gift	Archives
KL.1.2004.12.TL.46	**Dec. 2004**	Unsigned lyrics "Roadrunner's National Anthem"	Gift	Archives
KL.1.2004.12.VHS.1	**Dec. 2004**	April 10, 2004 A&E Special "City Confidential" 1979 battle between GSO activist and KKK	Gift	Archives
KL.1.2004.12.VHS.2	**Dec. 2004**	Feb. 5, 1985 KSU"Off Shoots" Presentation – The H.F. Lee family book By W.L. Fletcher w/ actual book	Gift	Archives

No Way!

CATALOG NUMBER	ACCESSION NUMBER	DECRIPTION	HOW ACQUIRED	MUSEUM LOCATION
KL.1.2004.12.VHS.3-4	Dec. 2004	1988 UNC Center for Public Television "Pitch a Boogie Woogie – Boogie in Black & White 58:45	Gift	Archives
KL.1.2004.12.YB.1	Dec. 2004	1952 year book Univ. of North Carolina at Chapel Hill	Gift	Archives
KL.2004.12.3D.1	Dec. 2004	9.5"x2" metal "Colored" sign removed from Guilford County Courthouse mid-1950's, signed letter form J. Kenneth Lee "It is placed here to remind us forever, of the "Way We Are"	Gift	**Courts and the Quest for Justice** Access Denied
KL.2004.12.3D.2	Dec. 2004	18"x12.5" black leather attaché case	Gift	**Courts and the Quest for Justice** Access Denied
KL.2004.12.3D.3	Dec. 2004	16"x13" black leather attaché case	Gift	**Courts and the Quest for Justice** Access Denied
KL.2004.12.3D.4	Dec. 2004	Silver and black 22 Derringer pistol no ammunition, box included	Gift	Archives
		BOX 3		
KL.3.2004.12.PQ.1	Dec. 2004	United States Court of Appeals Fourth Circuit 3-12-99. "Admitted and qualified as an Attorney and Counselor for the United States of Appeal."March 25, 1959	Gift	Gift
KL.3.2004.12.PQ.2	Dec. 2004	NC State A&T University the Faculty& Trustees have conferred Doctor of Laws.	Gift	Gift
KL.3.2004.12.PQ.3	Dec. 2004	Greensboro Bench and Bar Spouses for Selfless Contributions, February 1990.	Gift	Gift

CATALOG NUMBER	ACCESSION NUMBER	DECRIPTION	HOW ACQUIRED	MUSEUM LOCATION
		BOX 3		
KL.3.2004.12.PQ.4	Dec. 2004	State of North Carolina, Governor James E. Holshouser, Jr. Appointed as a member of the North Carolina Banking Commission August 15, 1980.	Gift	Gift
KL.3.2004.12.PQ.5	Dec. 2004	Honorable Discharge from the United States Navy as Electrician's Mate Second Class USNR on March 31, 1946. Shoemaker, California	Gift	Gift
KL.3.2004.12.PQ.6	Dec. 2004	Southeastern Lawyers Association certifies and duly qualified as a member of this Association on November 8, 1958.	Gift	Gift
KL.3.2004.12.PQ.7	Dec. 2004	The Agricultural and Technical College of North Carolina hereby confers the Degree of Bachelor of Science in Electrical Engineering on August 26, 1946.	Gift	Gift
KL.3.2004.12.PQ.8	Dec. 2004	The International Civil Rights Center & Museum presents Unsung Hero Award on Feb 1, 1995.	Gift	Gift
KL.3.2004.12.PQ.9	Dec. 2004	Junior Achievement of Guilford County, Inc. recognizes devotions to the free enterprise system and is selected as a member of the Greensboro Business Leaders Hall of Fame March 13, 1985.	Gift	Gift
KL.3.2004.12.PQ.10	Dec. 2004	The President, Professors and Board of Trustees of University of North Carolina have admitted to the Degree of Bachelor of Laws on August 22, 1958.	Gift	Gift

CATALOG NUMBER	ACCESSION NUMBER	DECRIPTION	HOW ACQUIRED	MUSEUM LOCATION
		BOX 3		
KL.3.2004.12.PQ.11	**Dec. 2004**	Board of Visitors of Greensboro College 1996.	Gift	Gift
KL.3.2004.12.PQ.12	**Dec. 2004**	North Carolina Housing Finance Agency	Gift	Gift
KL.3.2004.12.PQ.13	**Dec. 2004**		Gift	Gift
KL.3.2004.12.PQ.14	**Dec. 2004**	Hayes-Taylor YMCA honors In Grateful Appreciation for Outstanding and Distinguished Service.	Gift	Gift
KL.3.2004.12.PQ.15	**Dec. 2004**	Gate City Chapter welcomes Lifetime Member North Carolina A&T State University Alumni May 18, 1993.	Gift	Gift
KL.3.2004.12.PQ.16	**Dec. 2004**	The American Judicature Society certifies a member of the Society and supporter of its program to promote the Efficent Administration of Justice.	Gift	Gift
KL.3.2004.12.PQ.17	**Dec. 2004**	The State of North Carolina certifies that a license is hereby granted for the practice of Nursing Home Administration June 1, 1971.	Gift	Gift
Kl.3.2004.12.PQ.18	**Dec. 2004**	Chancellor's Council North Carolina Agricultural & Technical State University Greensboro this Award is made in appreciation for your continuous and generous support to student scholarship, faculty development and academic excellence.	Gift	Gift
Kl.3.2004.12.PQ.19	**Dec. 2004**	State of North Carolina Governor James G. Martin appoints as a member of the Housing Finance Agency Board of Directors June 30, 1989.	Gift	Gift

CATALOG NUMBER	ACCESSION NUMBER	DECRIPTION	HOW ACQUIRED	MUSEUM LOCATION
		BOX3		
Kl.3.2004.12.PQ.20	**Dec. 2004**	Greensboro Justice Fund Project Homestead Morningside Massacre Palque November 3, 1979	Gift	
Kl.3.2004.12.PQ.21	**Dec. 2004**	The University of North Carolina at Chapel Hill certifies and elect to Board of Visitors July 1, 1997 to June 30, 2001.	Gift	Gift
Kl.3.2004.12.PQ.22	**Dec. 2004**	Hamlet Public School District Colored School certifies a completed General Course of Study prescribed for the High School Department of Public Schools May 30, 1941.	Gift	Gift
Kl.3.2004.12.PQ.22	**Dec. 2004**	Hamlet Public School District Colored School certifies a completed General Course of Study prescribed for the High School Department of Public Schools May 30, 1941.	Gift	Archives
Kl.3.2004.12.PQ.23	**Dec. 2004**	Tax Court of the United States of North Carolina states the fulfilled requirements of this Court, having taken the oath and being duly qualified to the practice of the Tax Court of the United States November 11, 1968.	Gift	Archives
Kl.3.2004.12.PQ.24	**Dec. 2004**	The State of North Carolina this is to Certify that a Provisional License is hereby granted for the practice of Nursing Home Administration June 30, 1970.	Gift	Archives

CATALOG NUMBER	ACCESSION NUMBER	DECRIPTION	HOW ACQUIRED	MUSEUM LOCATION
		BOX 4		
KL.4.2004.12.PQ.1	Dec. 2004	John Davis of the Supreme Court of the United States of America, Greensboro, NC has admitted and qualified as an Attorney and Councelor of the Supreme	Gift	Archives
KL.4.2004.12.M.2	Dec. 2004	A& T State University Chancellor James C. Renick gives to honor courageous action against social injustice 2000.	Gift	Archives
KL.4.2004.12.PQ.3	Dec.2004	The North Carolina Housing Finance Agency Board of Directors and staff express appreciation and regard for the eight years of service to the North Carolina residents Dec 9, 1993.	Gift	Archive
KL.4.2004.12.PQ.4	Dec.2004	North Carolina Agricultural and Technical State University Alumni Association, Inc. Certificate of Appreciation for outstanding and dedicated service to your country while serving in WWII May 6, 1995.	Gift	Archive

ALL GIFT ITEMS RECEIVED FROM J. KENNETH LEE.

Author's Bio

Winona Lee Fletcher grew up as the last born in a large Southern family in North Carolina. Just out of college with a degree in English and Theatre she joined her brother, Kenneth, in his first business adventure--a Radio and Electronics School for veterans of WWII. After 3 years, her desire for further study in theatre overwhelmed her. Finding that the laws of segregation in her home state prohibited her access to higher education in her field, in 1950 she journeyed West where she later completed two advanced degrees--(M.A., Univ. of Iowa and Ph.D., Indiana Univ.) and never returned to the South. Between 1951 and 1994 she worked as teacher and administrator at universities in Kentucky, Missouri and Indiana.

She is a widow and professor emerita from both Kentucky State University and Indiana University where she was a professor of Theatre, Drama and Afro-American Studies for over 40 years. She lives in Frankfort, KY with frequent trips to Maryland to visit her daughter, son-in-law and granddaughter. At home, most of her time is spent preparing and transferring her vast collection of personal and professional materials to the archives at Kentucky State University's Center of Excellence for the Study of Kentucky African-Americans (CESKAA) and laughing with her brother as his ghostwriter and confidant over how much they have "forgotten to remember."

Printed in the United States
121442LV00003B